RAW SPIRIT

what the raw food advocates don't preach

Matthew J. Monarch

Layout & Design: Enrique Candioti
Cover Concept: Enrique Candioti

Library of Congress Catalog Card Number: on file
ISBN # 0-9769329-0-3
Copyright ©2005 by Matt Monarch
First Edition, October 2005

Monarch Publishing Company
12709 Byron Ave.,
Granada Hills, CA 91344
USA

Disclaimer:
This book is anecdotal of my experience. The following information
is for education only and is not meant to diagnose, prescribe, or
treat illness. It is valuable to seek the advice of an alternative
health care professional before making any changes.

ACKNOWLEDGEMENT

I would like to thank Michelle Sabathné for her invaluable contribution. She has the ability to turn the simplest words into artistic prose. Her inspiration and words of encouragement guided me throughout this endeavor. Her friendship has helped me throughout my journey. Thank you, Michelle, for all you have given of yourself.

CONTENTS

PART II

FOREWORD BY PAUL NISON

I am so pleased Matt has written this book. Through my own work I have met so many people who were struggling through the challenges of becoming Raw. It can be very confusing to make such a drastic change in diet; I have seen Matt go through numerous ups and downs. His reward for seeing it through and not giving up is the exceptional health he experiences today. He has gathered choice wisdom from many long time raw foodists and health advocates and offers his findings for you to make your health journey easier to understand.

As a bonus to Matt's inspiring testimonial and research, I am thrilled that he has decided to include an interview with Dr. Fred Bisci. I've met hundreds of people in the health field over the years and in my opinion, Dr. Bisci is the person whom I feel understands the most about health issues from a physical, emotional, and spiritual standpoint. The interview with Dr. Bisci in this book is outstanding and gives people the opportunity to learn from one of the most brilliant health minds of our time. I'm sure it will support and motivate many people on their quest for health.

It is because Matt has encountered and overcome these issues himself, prior to sharing them with others, that I am excited to write a forward for this book. Matt's testimonial and findings, along with Dr. Bisci's interview, makes Raw Spirit a very special resource and helpful guide for anyone interested in improving their quality of their health and life.

INTRODUCTION

Raw Food advocates preach the positives of becoming 100% Raw, painting a grand Garden of Eden existence. Without a doubt, the benefits of being Raw often cross into the realm of miraculous, yet not much light is cast on the whole picture. This book acknowledges the positives and goes on to detail the unspoken difficulties that commonly surface after a person takes the "big leap". In addition, interwoven within these pages is a subject rarely touched on by other books of this kind, that which I consider the most exciting reward of being Raw – the spiritual effect of a Raw Food diet.

The second part of Raw Spirit is an interview with a Master Nutritionist, Dr. Fred Bisci, someone I deem worthy of trust because of his experience in the field and his quality of character. It is because of Dr. Bisci's determination to help people get well and his 40 years on a Raw Diet that I am able to share with you the clearest, most accurate scientific explanation about why some diets heal and others *cannot*.

Elsewhere in the book you'll see drawings that illustrate what happens on a cellular level when one improves their diet; the most potent of these diets being the Raw Diet, which, as you will discover, is not a lifestyle to be taken lightly. Raw Spirit unveils the mystery about what goes on inside our bodies, making it possible to reclaim a level of health that has been lost to us.

OVERNIGHT

I went from 100% SAD (Standard American Diet) to 100% Raw in one day. This decision was not forced on me by illness, as I had no prior health concerns. Simply put, I was inspired. My inspiration was a book called *Become Younger* by Dr. Norman

Walker, who lived to be 118 years old. His book explained how to achieve health and longevity through a change in diet. He shared stories about people who had healed from every kind of disease and were now living exceptionally vibrant, long lives.

At the time I read Dr. Walker's book I felt young, active, and strong; even so, I saw the wisdom in his message and was excited that life could be even better for me now and into old age. It took me one night to finish his book and as I turned the last page, I knew I was closing the book on a part of my life that would never be the same. Over five years later, I am still eating only Raw Food.

Imagine, changing from a bachelor's diet of burgers, Subways, chicken patties and burritos to eating only raw vegetables, fruits, nuts, and seeds. I had no idea what was in store for me. This book describes my experiences, positive and negative, and offers you the wisdom of hindsight and a broader perspective. My intention is not to scare or excite you in any way, only to help prepare you for the journey.

WOULD I EVER GO BACK?

No! I would never go back to the way I used to eat. When people hear about my diet of raw fruits, vegetables, nuts and seeds they are usually shocked; it seems so strange and extreme. They strain to understand how I could still be existing, not to mention *thriving* on an all Raw Diet.

"Where do you get your protein?

What about calcium?

Must make it hard to travel.

Don't you get bored eating just vegetables?"

Many are merely curious, while others are impressed and want to know more. There are also those who give me a hard time; I think they try and find fault with my healthy diet to somehow justify their own food choices. Regardless of their intention, before we go our separate ways I think a part of them is touched by the diet's simplicity and a slightly buried admittance of how eating fresh, whole, raw foods just makes good common sense. My answer to most skeptical questions is usually in the form of a story. The following are a few of my favorites and they each involve Dr. Fred Bisci, who has been successfully Raw for over four decades.

During one of my visits to New York I was staying with Dr. Bisci at his home on Staten Island. Mid afternoon, we went to the boardwalk. As I struggled to keep pace with this 74 year old man, he drew my attention to the other people his age moving around us. Many of them had walkers and canes. He said, "Matt, the one thing you don't have to worry about when you become older is having to live inside a crippling body." If that isn't motivation, than I don't know what is. Later that year, Fred came to California for a visit and a few of us went on a hike. Now, I'm a pretty competitive man, but honestly, I couldn't keep up with the guy! Almost everyone I know his age, and even those ten years younger, have difficulty walking around the block. To them, it's exercise; to Fred, walking is a way to get to the beach so he can do his daily five mile run.

No, I will never go back to eating cooked food. When I first became Raw, amazing changes took place that proved to me I was on the right path and only made my commitment stronger. This next story is about one of those amazements. After working out in the gym, I would always head to the sauna for a cleansing sweat. On this particular day, when I stepped out of the sauna, I felt an instant clearing of my sinuses. As I breathed in through my nose, the air flew straight to my lungs without the slightest hint of congestion or stuffiness. Along with this new breath of life came a blast of energy. I had never felt so clean, so light; the feeling was weightlessness, my body felt like quickly moving energy rather than dense solid matter. I knew this was the way it should be, that everyone's body was made to feel this good all the time.

The newness and awe of this experience faded with time and as the months went by, I stopped appreciating my new state of health. It became my new 'normal'. One teaching of philosophy is that if you felt constant bliss and nothing else – no anger, grief, or struggle – you would not care for bliss any longer. If you had nothing to relate it to, no suffering for comparison, you would not know bliss as *bliss*.

Along those same lines, whenever I stray from my typical eating habits by overeating, poor food combining or overlapping meals, my body goes through unpleasant reactions; I fall from *bliss*, so to speak. This slip into suffering gives me a chance to revisit the newness of feeling good again. For example, sometimes I overeat fruit, which inevitably results in uncomfortable symptoms such as bloating, gas, depression and fatigue that can last for one to three days. Witnessing my body recover from the abuse, I can once again see the height from which I fell.

It's clear to me that if I returned to cooked food, I would not feel nearly as weightless and alive as I do now. In my mind, the benefits of a Raw Diet far outweigh anything that could be perceived as a loss. Being Raw was the best medicine my body could ever receive. Also, and much more exciting for me, was the profound spiritual transformation I underwent. As one's being flourishes from the 100% Raw Diet, they naturally open to the spiritual realities of life. You will read about a few of my "openings" in the Spiritual Rebirth chapter.

I BELONG ON ANOTHER PLANET

When I became a Raw Foodist my world got rocked upside down and inside out. I was alienated socially because of my unusual diet and because of the radical changes in my physical appearance. This may sound strange, but amidst all the physical side effects that were out of my control, I felt like a stranger in my own body; I was mad and confused at some of what I was having to endure. Feeling rejected on every front made it seem like *I belonged on another planet.*

I was born in the San Fernando Valley of California. Right out of college I moved to Santa Monica and took a job with MTV Networks. After two years, I requested a transfer to Time Square, NY. I was young, liked to party, and the move seemed like a good idea; which it was, until 2 1/2 years later when I became Raw and had to escape the city smog.

First, let me talk about the social craziness that happened immediately following my change in diet. My eating was so skewed from what most considered normal and acceptable that many saw me as weird or freakish.

Looking back, I can understand their perspective. After all, I did drop over 20 pounds in a single month once I became Raw. I looked quite shocking, mostly, believe it or not, because my new body did not match my old hairstyle. For years my hairstyle had been a short cropped cut with closely shaven sides. When I went in for my usual weekly trim, the barber turned the chair around and I was shocked to see a skeleton looking back at me. Because of my weight loss, having my sides shaven so close made me look much too thin. I've been growing my hair long since that day.

Around the same time, I got a call from an old friend I'd known since junior high who was also living in New York. We stayed in touch, though it was about a month since we had last seen each other. Keep in mind, it was practically overnight that I lost those 20 pounds. Imagine seeing someone one week and then meeting with a 20 lb. lighter version of him three weeks later. Since I was not carrying much extra weight to begin with, the change to my features was startling. When we met for lunch, I saw her heart drop. She was obviously worried, to say the least. That experience left me daunted and a little concerned about how my family in California would react; they had not seen me in over a year. What would their reactions be and what about all my other friends back home, what would they think?

Despite the drama I knew I was walking into, going back to my old diet was not an option. Alone, dizzily walking the streets of New York, I was immersed in the temptation of smells from foods and restaurants, passing pizza joints and sushi bars on every block, yet there was no turning back. Unfortunately, my fears about others' reactions came to fruition and most of my family and friends pulled away from me. Some of my family needed over four years to be truly accepting. You may need to be prepared for a social knockout!

When someone witnesses a massive change from the reality they knew, from the you they knew, they may pull back. Their energy of fear and confusion can be contagious, causing you to feel self-conscious and unsure about the path you've chosen. With those I had known *before* my switch to Raw, this was certainly the pattern. However, my interactions with strangers were refreshingly opposite. One of my more flashy examples happened while walking home from work in Time Square when a stylishly dressed business woman stopped me on the street. "Have you ever thought about modeling?" She handed me a business card, inviting me to call her company if I was ever interested. The truth of the matter is that your appearance takes on a divine essence while on a Raw Diet. Your facial features become more defined, your skin glows, and your spiritual energy vibrates at an almost tangible rate. You become gorgeous.

SOCIALIZING

People are always curious to know *if* and *how* I ever go out to eat with my friends and family. Dining out is a universally popular element of socializing, especially with my family who love to gather and share meals for any and all occasions, either at home or out. There's no way I would want to miss all the fun so I do one of two things: eat nothing or bring my own food. Restaurants are accustomed to people with special diets and I've found most to be very lenient and accommodating, although I seldom get away without raising a few eyebrows.

Dining out brings me to another closely related social challenge: group gatherings. It has been five years since I turned Raw and yet people who have known this fact for quite some time are still intrigued. It never fails that my diet becomes the main topic of discussion, at least for an uncomfortable little while. I can appreciate how being Raw is an easy target for conversation, and have come to accept it. Usually, I handle the interrogation well, fielding questions amidst mouthfuls of salad. Nevertheless, their probing sometimes makes me feel like I belong on another planet.

One of the most popular excuses for not going Raw is the social ramifications. Having lived through it, I can assure you the rewards make it well worth the sacrifices. Leaving the mainstream to go on a less traveled path is a spiritual journey. It opens your eyes to see things in a new light and you stop being affected by our culture's bad influences – poor food choices, smoking, drinking, and ignorance about your body's needs. Excuses to not go Raw are usually nonsense. There is just one thing you need to be concerned about and that is your *commitment*. As long as your commitment is strong, nothing can stop you.

PHYSICAL CHANGES

The single most important piece of information that Dr. Fred Bisci ever passed on to me has never been taught before. Simply said, the lesson is this: When someone becomes a 100% raw food eater, his or her chemistry completely changes on a cellular level. Let me explain why understanding this one thing can make such a difference.

If you are not 100% Raw at this time, imagine for a moment that you are:

Welcome to the twilight zone. You belong on another planet. You have eliminated from your diet everything except raw fruits, vegetables, nuts, and seeds. Your previous diet, that likely included an excess of cooked and/or processed foods, has clogged and obstructed your tissues, cells, airways, pores, organs, and bloodstream to one degree or another. Day after day, your body was forced to find some way to use and dispose of those less then ideal foods. Conversely, on your new 100% Raw Diet, the strenuous time-consuming demand of digesting cooked and processed food is gone. The hard working body is now free to do other things, and this is when the magic begins. Your body, on a cellular level, starts to change.

You are made of cells. Everything that you see externally like skin, hair, and nails, are cells. And every-thing being housed inside you such as organs, muscle, tissue, bone, and blood are also made up of differently grouped cells. Because every part of you is composed of cells, it is very significant that when you switch to a Raw Diet, your body, on a cellular level, completely changes. Your overly fed, con-gested, unclean cells can finally clean house  and start to dispose of all their endogenous material – the buildup of waste and gas inside a cell. As months go by, you become cleaner and cleaner. Disposing of this toxic matter causes your cells to shrink and contract, and they con-tinue to become tighter and tighter.

Sounds great, right? I of course agree, but I also need to point out that becoming clean and tight on a cel-lular level has consequences.

Once you leave out all obstruction causing foods for a good amount of time (as you automatically do on a Raw Diet), your body refuses to accept anything less than what it is now accustomed to. To use an example, you may have heard stories about vegetarians or vegans who tried to eat meat after years of abstinence. The result: the body rejects it

and they become ill; now you will understand why. Meat causes obstruction and toxicity in the body and by omitting this food *completely*, the vegetarian's body was given the chance to become tighter on a cellular level. After the span of abstinence, meat was seen as a foreign enemy and the body's reaction was simply an unwillingness to revert to its prior state of toxicity. Previously, their oversized, unclean cells were able to handle the meat, but as a vegetarian, the now cleaner, tighter cells, could not.

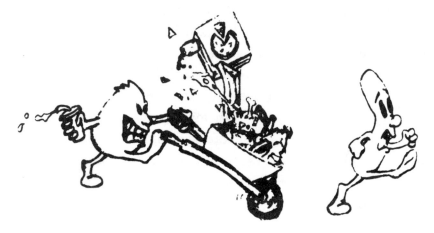

Let us look deeper into the adaptation abilities of the body. It is common knowledge that if you get bit by a venomous snake, your life expectancy goes down considerably, from many years to perhaps only a few precious minutes. The poison in venom has the power to kill because it is foreign to the body on a cellular level. There are proven stories, of snake hunters that use the adaptation powers of the body to become immune to this poison. By introducing small amounts of venom into their blood stream, a drop or two at a time, they gradually increase the dosage until they can handle as much as a single snakebite or two. (I do not recommend this, as your body will suffer in the long run.)

In this culture, we too are snake hunters of some sort. Feeding an infant what many of us eat in a typical day would be their demise. Yet little by little, bite by bite, as the years of our lives go by, we manage to build up quite a tolerance. As adults, it took a lifetime for our cells to adapt to a level of accepting and handling all the foods we eat. (And, like the snake hunter, our bodies suffer in the long run.) There is hope. On a Raw Diet, it can take only a few months to a year for our cells to reach a cleaner, tighter state. This means, however, that we will no longer be able to handle the poisons from our previous diet.

When you are 100% Raw, your body becomes clean and vulnerable, like the snake hunter before he introduced the venom or an infant before the double burger with cheese. In this clean and vulnerable state, one of the worst things a Raw Foodist can do is go back and forth between a raw diet and a cooked diet. Yo-yoing at this stage is so unhealthy in fact, that it would be better to never become Raw in the first place.

It is something to think about before you make the switch. Perhaps an intermediate, 80% Raw lifestyle would be perfect for you. I give this warning because Raw foods move the body ahead so fast that you may get stuck at a level you do not want to be at. At the stage my body and cells are at now, it would take many months to safely transition back into even the more healthy cooked foods. Many people I talk to can't quite understand or accept that the foods they eat everyday would almost definitely land me in the hospital.

ONE COMMON DENOMINATOR

All those who know Dr. Fred Bisci are very familiar with the next sentence you are about to read. "It is what you leave out of your diet *completely* that heals you." Many popular diets such as, *The Macrobiotic Diet, The Maker's Diet, The Blood Type Diet*, and so on, have produced positive results. Close up they seem very different and it may be hard to choose which is best. Here is a little secret that will simplify things considerably: *They are all the same!* They all have one common denominator, one secret weapon that deserves the credit for all their success. It is this: Their diet protocols require one to abstain from certain food groups, *completely*. For example, all processed starches, junk foods, and refined sugar, are "no no's". The Raw Diet is the most thorough in this regard and therefore the most effective for healing because it leaves out every obstruction causing food known to man.

The main point being illustrated here is that *one does not experience health because of what they eat, they heal because of what they **do not** eat*. I know several people with health issues. Sadly, most people's efforts to improve their condition are identical. They eat more vegetables and usually take some sort of daily fiber supplement. If I cross paths with a misdirected mind like this, he or she may pridefully flaunt their plate full of vegetables; yet my attention is on the slab of steak and side of fries also sharing a space on their plate, or whatever I may catch a glimpse of them sneaking from the fridge later that night. I roll my eyes and want to scream, "It is what you *don't* do that heals you!" I don't care if they eat vegetables and raw foods until they are blue in the face, because I understand that they are not going to get better unless they stop eating the foods that got them sick in the first place.

Obviously extreme, but making his point, Fred often says to people, "If all you ate was dead rats, you'd get healthier because of the fact that you're leaving everything else out." From a more realistic perspective, even if all your meals were cooked, but only consisted of fruit, vegetables, nuts and seeds, your chemistry would improve dramatically because of what you are *not* eating.

PROCESS OF ELIMINATION

From what I've seen, being Raw is much more effective for health than being Vegetarian. If I was not Raw, and instead chose to follow an intermediate diet for health, meat is the last thing I would eliminate. First things to go completely would be the refined sugar, starch, and then dairy. The cellular health of vegetarians that abstain from meat, yet eat freely of the other junk foods, are far from the level of a Raw Foodist.

It is what you *don't* eat that heals you. It is what you leave out of your diet COMPLETELY, with no cheating. This "no cheating" piece is imperative. I've had frequent experiences with people saying they ate all Raw for a year and it didn't help them with their degenerative disease. Immediately, I know why they failed. I have seen it happen over and over again. My first question to them is, "Did you ever cheat?" They hesitate and say, "Maybe once a month I would have this or that." If you do not leave something out of your diet *completely*, your body does not have the freedom to go to the next level. Throwing the body into trauma every other week with cooked or processed foods is enough to keep it in a constant state of repair.

Tighter, cleaner cells make us more sensitive to foods. This level of cleanliness also makes us vulnerable to environmental factors. As mentioned earlier, I started my Raw lifestyle in New York City. Every morning on my walk to work, I would swim thru a thick sea of vehicles and machinery blowing their dark clouds of pollution into the air. And for the entire length of this daily death march I was elbow to elbow in a herd of cigarette smoking people. (It must be that at least 75% of New Yorkers smoke cigarettes.)

Before my switch to Raw, I had no problem during the trek to work and would walk, head held high, my thoughts buzzing about the upcoming day. Yet that ease and ignorance was yanked away once my cellular structure changed. I felt like the very air was killing me. Truth be told, it was killing me. Pollution harms a raw food eater more than the average person. Similar to the example of the snake hunter, because I was cleaner and tighter on a cellular level, my body could not handle the venom of pollution. My distance to work was now a mission of survival, a never winning warfare. It involved crossing the street probably twenty times, seeking safe passage in the least polluted spots I could find, dodging cigarette smokers, and feeling attacked from all sides.

My struggle with pollution is the sole reason I left New York City. Unfortunately, air pollution is hard to avoid in this day and age and the thought once again surfaced, *I feel like I belong on another planet.* I wanted to relocate to a place closer to my family and was able to find a bit of clean air in a small town near Santa Barbara, where I still live today.

HOW CAN I DO THE RAW DIET RIGHT?!?

How can I do Raw right? Becoming Raw is a serious undertaking and following the wrong path could lead to problems in the long run, as it has for some. This fact should by no means stop us from journeying, though it does inspire a certain respect for raw foods.

There are numerous convincing and brilliant theories from many well-intentioned, remarkable individuals. Rigidly following any one person's ideas is just not smart, in my opinion. I recommend gathering an enormous mass of information from as many books and people as you can and applying the tidbits that intuitively make you feel great. My personal eating and lifestyle is based on a combination of wisdom I adopted from a few of the greats including Dr. Norman Walker, Dr. Fred Bisci, Arnold Ehret, Paul Nison, Hilton Hotema, Dr. St. Louis Estes, Bernard Jenson, and others. I apply what intuitively and experimentally makes me feel GREAT.

Where do you start? Listen to your body. It is easy to ignore the body because it does not demand full obedience. Our body gives us a choice and holds out the best it can until we choose to pay attention and follow its gentle lead. If you tune into your body there's always a clue, a hint, that's being shown in the form of discomfort, pain, or decreased well-being when some food or behavior is not in your best interest.

The earlier you pay attention and follow, the better. Let's say you eat mainly fruit all day long for many years. Your body can and will eventually adapt to that diet and feel fine after awhile. But although fruit is wonderful to eat in *moderation*, excess fruit eating will eventually cause worsening symptoms of ill-health as the body attempts to hail your attention, before it's too late.

TOO MUCH FRUIT

I have heard some unfortunate stories about people whose diets had consisted of mainly fruit for many years. Under such conditions they start to show signs of dis-ease in the body including hair loss, tooth erosion, and osteoporosis. One might think all the fruit sugar is what ruins the teeth, when in actuality it is the high quantity of mineral loss from such a diet that causes them to erode.

Also, when one eats too much fruit, the body must produce large amounts of insulin to counter the raise in blood sugar levels. This condition is called *hyperinsulin*. The chemical imbalance of hyperinsulin can lead to worsening conditions including irritability, frequent urination, arterial damage, and hypoglycemia. Too much sugar also causes fermentation, which is disastrous to the body. Furthermore, one cannot possibly "connect all the dots", as Fred would say; one cannot receive the full spectrum of nutrients their body needs without a good variety of raw foods. And, if you recall, the chemistry of a raw food eater is much different from that of a cooked food eater. Too much fruit is not good for anyone, although it will affect and hurt a Raw Foodist more severely because they are cleaner and tighter on a cellular level.

All in all, becoming 100% Raw has its roses and its thorns. On the rosy end, you have increased sensitivity with immediate noticeable feedback from your body as to what it wants and what would be best to avoid. On the thorny flipside, there is minimal margin for error, which causes many problems for the raw food eater that I will soon discuss.

One thing I'm certain of is that the body was probably giving those who overate fruit some pretty urgent alerts prior to osteoporosis and hair loss. If they were paying conscious attention to their bodies, the symptoms would not have progressed so far. When I eat a lot of sugar fruit, my body tells me to STOP. I start to smell bad; I become jittery; my teeth ache; I get uncomfortable gas; my nose runs; I move at what feels like 1000 miles per hour; and, I feel dirty inside. If I were to persist and continue eating those same amounts of fruit, my body's objections would be silenced, yet in the long run I would have to answer for that abuse.

Everyone's body and chemistry are different. By no means do I think there is one right way to follow the Raw Diet. The information I'm offering is just a piece, and hopefully a helpful one. My advice will always be to gather as much information as possible and ultimately, to simply listen to your own body.

TOO MUCH FAT

You've learned one can adapt to overeating sugary fruit, and the same is true for excessive fat consumption. Raw fat is *IN*; if it's Raw and it's fat, you can eat it – avocados, coconuts, nuts, olives – and you don't have to stop! Although it is not as harmful as overeating fruit, too much fat in the blood is not good either.

I like to use Norman Walker as an example because he lived to be 118 years old; he was obviously doing something right. His entire day's fat intake would often be half an avocado and a small amount of nuts. Dr. Walker's body was definitely not overburdened with fat, and he had sufficient food to give him a long and healthy life. I am not recommending the "Norman Walker way", although a diet similar to Norman Walker's is a personal goal of mine. In his diet, he mastered one of the biggest keys to longevity: systematic undereating; and I go into more detail about that soon.

DON'T GET FANATICAL

There's no need to get fanatical. Often I hear people in the Raw community preaching that to be truly healthy you should never go to Raw Food restaurants, or eat things like *Bragg's Liquid Aminos, Noma Shoyu,* and dehydrated foods. Although I applaud their passion, to me, that viewpoint is too black and white. If you are replacing processed junk food with prepared Raw Food, you are doing great. You are healing. It is what you *do not* eat that heals you. It is what you leave out of your diet COMPLETELY that moves you forward.

Let me also say here that committing to 100% Raw is not necessary to dramatically improve the condition of your cells. If you leave out all the processed junk (anything that comes in a box), refined sugar, flours, dairy, and so on, you will become cleaner on a cellular level. As your cellular structure continues to purify itself, your body will naturally start to reject any remaining foods still in your diet that are less than ideal for perfect health and longevity. Currently, my body has a rough time accepting some of what I used to eat when I first became Raw, including food prepared at Raw restaurants and dehydrated foods. So I don't eat them, and that is what works best for me.

You can't go wrong if you listen to your body. It is a process of elimination. When something makes you feel poorly, it's usually time to stop eating it. If you are not sure what is making you feel bad, experiment by removing foods from your diet until you can pinpoint the culprit. Also, rely on your intuitive sense for guidance. If you don't want to eliminate whatever is causing the discomfort, then accept the runny nose, digestive discomfort, or slight fatigue, and move on. At some point there's a great chance you will grow beyond it, and there is little permanent gain made by forcing anything.

TRANSITIONING

When you first become 100% Raw, it is expected that you will not be in perfect balance with your food choices. Depending on your previous eating habits, you may need weeks, months, or even years of overeating raw foods until your body and detoxification normalize. After being Raw for a sufficient amount of time, you will be ready to take on more responsibility.

When you first convert, it can be a little bit crazy. I remember meeting an older overweight man who had just turned Raw a few months prior. He was leaving everything out of his diet except raw fruits, vegetables, nuts, and seeds. At one point during the gathering I was at, he confessed to our group that he eats a jar of almond butter every day, gets knocked out from all the fat and protein, and then falls asleep. In spite of his almond butter habit, this man was losing massive amounts of weight and healing his body. I was thrilled to hear the advice given to him: "You are doing great! Keep up the good work. Who cares if you eat a jar of almond butter a day and fall asleep? Eventually that impulse will be gone. For now, eat all the almond butter you want."

In my own saga, I made the decision to switch to 100% Raw overnight. What followed was a far from perfect transition. At the time, the only book I had ever read on the subject was by Dr. Norman Walker. I followed his menu plans as a guide. Looking back on it now, I realize that my meals didn't even come close to the outline he gave. My quantities for lunch and dinner were at least quadruple those he recommended. For instance, a typical day's menu for me included drinking up to five 16-24 oz. vegetable juices a day. And I can still remember the wild looks from people walking by my office at MTV Networks seeing me enjoying four large avocados and four pounds of grapes for lunch. Once at home I would feast on a huge salad with avocado cucumber dressing. After the last bite of salad I would start on a pound or two of wet, fat, succulent dried figs. I was tired, knocked out, and had no idea why.

At the end of this book, I will discuss exactly what my diet is like currently, now that the normalizing period has passed.

THIS TOO SHALL PASS

When you become 100% Raw, your chemistry on a cellular level completely changes. This concept is of such superior importance for any Raw Foodist that it cannot be said enough. If you have been Raw for more than a year, your body is so completely different that it is accurate to say you are no longer the person you used to be.

When I ate the Standard American Diet, quantities and cravings were never an issue for me. After I became Raw, the ease of mindless eating vanished and in its place appeared many imbalances and stresses around eating. If handled with a healthy awareness, these experiences can be no big deal. It is possible you may breeze through and not have any issues come up along your journey. However, if you are faced with a challenge, realize that this is expected and is only temporary. Just as the older gentleman from last chapter will not be eating a jar of almond butter everyday for the rest of his life, you will not get stuck either.

When I was going through the worst of my food issues, I knew that any imbalanced habits were only temporary and had to be waited out; somehow I knew I could trust the process. What I am about to reveal, I have not shared with many people. Disclosing my low times with others may have stirred people's judgment or worry for something they simply could not understand.

Caution: If you feel you need the support of family, friends, or an alternative health care practitioner, please do not hesitate.

DREAMING ABOUT FOOD

The first issue that arose for me around food is very common. I used to think incessantly about food, non-stop daydreams and imaginings so real I would start to salivate. I was practically living just so I could eat. My brain felt like it was watching a tennis match, continually lifting my head from work to check the time, waiting for the clock to strike: EAT! To restrain my ferocious appetite I would target a specific time in my head and commit to waiting until then for my next meal. Even though I had the willpower to wait, I was very impatient for the time I could once again enjoy stuffing myself.

My menu for the entire week was planned ahead. At the Farmers' Market I would count out the exact amount of figs or persimmons I needed to last the week. Everyone in the house knew not to touch my stash of food. Only recently have I parted with the "MINE" syndrome. Evidently, some changes take longer than others.

Food's grip on me has loosened; these days I no longer dream about food and I have balance with quantity, desiring to only eat when I'm hungry. Obsessive hang-ups are typical among individuals beginning a Raw lifestyle.

OVEREATING

Overeating can be the slipperiest obstacle to surpass. Eating cooked food versus raw food is a colossally different experience psychologically, emotionally, and physically. Raw food leaves you satisfied, more nourished than your body has ever been, and it can accomplish this with very little quantity. However, raw food does not give you that stuffed sensation the same way cooked food does, unless you overeat. And when you overeat raw food, watch out! Be ready to deal with some uncomfortable digestive upsets.

It took me years to balance out. At first, I overate everyday. Months and months went by and every night after eating my "Super Size Me" salad, I would fall asleep reclining on the couch, but not before making several trips to and from the kitchen for more food. The truth is that the overeating was out of my control and I had tremendous guilt and judgment watching myself turn into an eating madman.

What a nasty feeling guilt is, far worse for me than the actual act of overeating. It would be much easier to simply acknowledge and accept that you are attempting to do something tremendous that will have far reaching rewards. Realize a transition period is expected as you forge your way into this new lifestyle.

Believe me, I paid for my excesses. Overeating on fruit was disastrous! I would eat one persimmon and then another and another until I had gobbled down 15 of them. The result of overeating fruit is much worse than overeating salad. My digestive system would be a mess for two days. My gas was so copious and rank that I had to avoid public places. You would think symptoms like these would be enough incentive for me to never overeat again. The problem with something out of your control, is that you don't have a choice.

My mentors, those who had gone through this transition themselves, calmed my worries by saying that my body and emotions were adjusting and needed time. I would say it takes a minimum of three years to comfortably settle into being Raw.

EATING DISORDERS

"Never! I will never overeat again!" was the promise I made at many different points throughout my Raw Food history. But, as I found out, that promise was never really mine to make. My over consumption of fruit eventually escalated to an eating disorder similar to bulimia. The amount of times that I fell subject to an extreme like this were few, although it did happen.

Persimmons are one of my favorite fruits. They are about the size of an apple and depending on their ripeness, about eight times sweeter. If I at one persimmon, everything was fine. Four persimmons, and there was no turning back; I had already gone over the edge. As the sugar blasts into my blood stream I crave more, I start to shake. My spun out emotions and body take complete control over my meager will power, which was just an illusion anyway. Before I know it, I'm in the kitchen with the whole mother load of persimmons. "No! I don't want to overeat! I don't want gas and tiredness!" In desperation I would take a persimmon, walk over to the trash, chew it, and then spit it out. Unable to stop I would go and take another and another, again and again. Then I would break out the dried figs, chew them up, and spit out into the trash, one fig, three figs, ten figs. The stress, shame, and shock over my behavior were overwhelming. I was reeling, feeling crazy and almost psychotic. These crashes into binging would usually occur after a few weeks of eating really well, probably just as my body was beginning to throw off large amounts of toxic material to push into a new level of cleanliness.

It gets worse. Farmers' Markets are scattered all over southern California and it was not unusual for me to drive an hour or more to get to my precious fruit. These Markets are like huge sugar fruit smorgasbords and for a guy like me I would head for it like a man possessed. And of course, once I arrived, I would ridiculously overeat on fresh succulent fruit that had been hand harvested only a few hours before. Fresh, organic, in season – Oooohhh, it was *so good!* On the drive home, however, I would be face to face with digestive discomfort, and anger over what I did. In pure disgust and disappointment I began belching, and the fruit in my stomach would be forced up into my mouth. Belch and spit, belch and spit.

The chemicals released into our bodies from guilt are physiologically worse than the overeating itself. Watch out for that. Also, be prepared because when you become a 100% raw food eater, buried emotional issues may surface. One reason for this is because when you don't have food to medicate yourself, life gets real, very quickly.

Variations of the experiences and extremes I shared are common for the raw food eater that is just starting out. I encourage you to stick with it. At some point you will need to come into balance in order to reap the full benefits of being Raw. If your commitment is strong, then your journey will be quite phenomenal.

BAD FOOD COMBINATIONS

Food combining is based on the premise that certain foods digest well when eaten together, while others should not be eaten in the same meal to ensure good breakdown and assimilation. For example, proteins should not be eaten with sugars or starches; fruits do best eaten alone and before other foods; and so on. These rules are determined by differing digestion speeds and particular digestive chemistry activated in the body for each food group.

When I ate cooked food, bad food combinations never caused any noticeable side effects. Now, my leash is much tighter and the slightest miscombination results in a large quantity of gas, among other annoying symptoms. One of the reasons for this acute reaction is because the live enzymes in raw food make digestion a more concise quick process; there is no sluggishness or sludgy byproducts to make symptoms go unnoticed. Also, as a cooked food eater, my body did not have the vitality to respond quickly enough or forcefully enough for me to notice.

Just like the vegetarian who can't eat meat anymore without getting sick, as time goes on and you keep improving your diet and lifestyle, you become "locked in" to certain habits such as food combining, the size of your meals, not eating late at night, and so on. This process of getting "locked in" happens quickly. Your body has no processed foods to work on so all its energy is focused on improving your internal chemistry; your cells become tighter and cleaner at an exponential rate.

MEDICAL DRUGS, RECREATIONAL DRUGS, CIGARETTES, AND ALCOHOL

The chemistry and condition of one who has lived Raw for many years has reached a level of unparalleled sensitivity. What scares me the most about being Raw long-term is our increasing vulnerability to concentrated chemicals that in this day and age are used in minor surgeries, routine medical testing, and emergency procedures. When someone gets into a nasty car accident or medical emergency, doctors often use intravenous drugs in treatment. For the long-term 100% Raw

Foodist, those concentrated chemicals can present a problem.

Here is a comparison: a person doing narcotics for 15 years has built up a certain tolerance and can handle much more than an individual trying them for the first time. In much the same way, a Raw Foodist is like a first time user. But the drug in this case is not crack or heroine; it is Western medicine.

What about raising children Raw? Imagine that you have a 10 year old child who has been 100% Raw since birth. He would be so clean and tight on a cellular level that it could be dangerous for him. Let's say, for example, that he just met some new friends and is tempted to eat a hamburger. One or two bites and he may end up in the hospital. Raw children must be well educated about how their chemistry is different from the mass majority. And what about the possibility of your child in a car accident? If your Raw Foodist son or daughter was given a concentrated chemical such as morphine, there is a possibility that he or she could experience serious side effects.

There are special medical tags that withhold permission for use of hospital drugs. I have one that I wear around my neck, it reads: *anaphylactic to pharmaceutical and intravenous drugs*. Wearing this tag is a serious choice with life or death consequences. One would not want to revoke medical assistance unless they were sure their body was at the point where it would do more harm then good. 99% of those reading this book will not need to wear a medical tag. *Although I want to share all the information I can, I do not and cannot accept liability for anyone who may choose to withhold permission for use of hospital drugs.*

What about pets? The same rules of sensitivity apply to

pets on an all Raw Diet. I just heard a story recently about a man and his dog. The poor dog was limping and had cyst-like bumps all over his skin, both signs indicating an overly toxic system. The Veterinarian said the dog's leg would need to be amputated. Desperate for an alternative, the man started feeding his dog all raw foods, including raw meat. On this 100% Raw Diet, the dog was back to normal in no time, and all the bumps disappeared. The man continued feeding his dog raw foods and many years later when the animal needed to be brought in for age related problems, the Veterinarian suggested a drug that might help. Even though the man didn't feel good about it, he gave his permission. A few hours later, the dog died.

We all know that recreational drugs such as marijuana, cigarettes, and alcohol are not good for us. For someone that eats a Raw Diet, the harmful effects from these types of drugs are multiplied. If someone has a chronic substance addiction or habit, it is best for him or her to *not* become 100% Raw until they are through their addictions.

I met a woman the other day who was a chain smoking Raw Foodist. She doesn't realize how much more harmful smoking is for her than the average person. If I were her, I would choose to either quit smoking or stop being 100% Raw. In my own experience, it's painfully obvious that being around cigarette smoke hurts me a great deal more now then when I ate cooked food. When I became a Raw Foodist I stopped partying. Honestly, I just lost the taste for it. I remember the first drink of alcohol I had after becoming Raw. It was a small glass of natural, organic red wine. I didn't get tipsy or drunk; I got *ill*. My body can no longer handle alcohol, even if I wanted it to.

COLONICS

The two key elements in health are eating a good diet and having sufficient elimination. You need both for optimal health and healing. As I discussed earlier, when you embark on a diet of only raw foods, your cells finally have enough energy to unburden themselves of their accumulated waste, which they immediately start to release into your blood stream for elimination. The best way to keep up with all the junk being dumped into your system is by doing colonics.

This is a subject I am very passionate about because one of the main reasons many people fail on a Raw Diet is their inability to rid themselves of this age old waste matter fast enough. Keep in mind this sudden load of extra toxins is not all the body must eliminate. There is also the daily massive amount of waste being released into your system from normal cell metabolism, environmental toxins, and digestion. Result: the body simply can't keep up; you start feeling lousy, blame the diet, and then quit. It is my opinion, and that of many experienced health minds, that people on a healing or Raw Diet would have more success if they did colonics two to three times a month, especially when they first begin eating differently.

Keeping your body and intestines clean is imperative for longevity. Dr. Norman Walker lived to be well over 100 and although not quite 100% Raw, he was heavy into juicing and colonics. I feel, as did he, that colonics were one of the main reasons he lived to be 118. Colonics allowed him to keep up with the waste matter being dumped into his system from his purging cells.

Although colonics can help anyone and everyone, I believe they are especially advantageous for the individual taking steps to improve his or her diet indefinitely. This is because if you clean your colon of waste without improving your diet, you eventually end up where you started.

Waste matter allowed to stay in the body, delivers a punch. These toxins can cause insatiable cravings, feelings of being sick, and mood swings that depress your excitement about improving your diet. A colonic relieves your system of this waste; if you'll forgive the comparison, it's like flushing the toilet.

"Flushing" out this build up of internal waste takes the burden off your body, and it immediately starts to work on your internal chemistry. For someone traveling the road to health, colonics can help catapult your wellness to the next level.

Gas and waste were my biggest annoyances just starting out on the Raw Diet. When the pressure and back-up reached a certain point of discomfort, I would schedule a colonic. After the colon cleansing I felt clean, light, and full of energy. The word that comes to mind is *ecstasy*. This heightened state would slowly dwindle down over a period of 7 to 10 days. Then, once again, I would be overrun with gas and waste; the gas made being in public very embarrassing and the waste had me feeling heavy and depressed, not to mention the added bother of a runny nose and zits. Horrible. Off to the colon therapist, and again magically teleported to the top of the world. My sinuses cleared immediately and my acne vanished overnight. Lying in bed, I felt *blissful*.

I had questions. Why didn't I have problems with waste and gas on my cooked food diet? Why do I have them now that I am Raw and eating healthier than ever before? Quite a few therories surfaced. Some people I asked weren't sure what the problem was, but believed in the power of raw foods and encouraged me to trust what was happening. Others thought I was experiencing fast paced detoxification. We also entertained the idea that I was just drinking too much vegetable juice. Great answers; I saw truth in them all.

It may surprise you to know that five years later, I am still asking the same questions and suffering similar complaints. Granted, the symptoms are much more diluted and I don't need to do a colonic every week, but I still have occasional annoyances like a runny nose and intestinal gas. I function best with one or two colonics per month.

Frequent colonic appointments can get fairly pricey, so I started looking for cheaper alternatives that could deliver similar results. My search brought me to something called a *Colema Board®*. Unlike a colonic, a colema can be self-administered and done right at home. For me, my first colema meant my last colonic. Dr. Bernard Jensen, a popular nutritionist and author of many health books, highly recommends the use of a colema board. It is a necessary element for his famous seven day psyllium and bentonite deep tissue cleanse. Soon after my colema board discovery, I did a slightly altered version of his cleanse and two days later started feeling an intense, almost tangible vibration in my forehead. I will go into more detail about this sensation in the Spiritual Rebirth chapter.

If you choose to do Dr. Bernard Jenson's psyllium bentonite cleanse, know that the power of this protocol will change your body's level of health. It is a seven day cleanse without solid food. Two specially designed drinks are taken five times a day with supplements. Colemas are done morning and evening each day of the cleanse. If you choose to, you can literally see the age old waste as it comes out. The amount of incrusted waste released from my system was jaw dropping shocking!

The psyllium bentonite protocol is a very advanced and very doable cleanse, fully capable of thoroughly dewasting your system. For best results I recommend this cleanse after a three to six month improved diet that includes drinking green vegetable juices and omitting all processed foods. The improvement in your diet along with the green vegetable juice allows your body to begin the process of eliminating all the incrusted waste clogging each and every cell, organ, and tissue throughout your system. Results you obtain from a cleanse done after the three months will be considerable.

Dr. Bernard Jensen's book, which details the seven day cleanse, is *Tissue Cleansing Through Bowel Management*. He recommends a few supplements; Cod liver oil is not Raw vegan, so you must decide for yourself about some of what he prescribes. The most important products to use are psyllium and bentonite. When I did the seven day cleanse I replaced supplements with a simple green juice and still achieved amazing results. My body was more sensitive by this time and didn't need as much support from supplements to deep cleanse.

ARE COLONICS SAFE?

Cleansing the colon is an important practice that everyone can benefit from. Some are against colonics because they seem unnatural. Others say that flushing the colon with water can wash away healthy bacteria. Dr. Norman Walker, an expert in the field of colon health, puts to rest these fears in his writings. He starts by saying very matter-of-factly that some things people believe just aren't true.

The other important function of the first half of the colon is to gather from the glands in its walls the intestinal flora needed to lubricate the colon. Far too many people, professional and laymen, think that enemas and colon irrigations wash out the intestinal flora and thus deprive the colon of a valuable means of lubrication. This school of thought is utterly false and totally devoid of truth and fact.

He goes on in passionate voice to make clear why colon cleansing is absolutely necessary and how a dirty compacted colon is the main culprit responsible for all symptoms of ill health. Disease begins in the colon and any efforts for healing will ultimately fail if the colon is not addressed.

Obviously, when the packed accumulation of feces in the bowel leads to fecal incrustation, it is not possible for the lining of the colon to function normally...

The fecal incrustation interferes with, if it does not actually prevent, (1) the infusion of the necessary intestinal flora for colon lubrication, [promoting constipation and toxemia from old fecal matter remaining in the body] (2) the formation of peristaltic waves for evacuation purposes, and (3) the absorption and use of the additional nutritional elements present in the waste residue coming into the colon from the small intestine.

The colon is a natural breeding ground for bacteria. There are two types of bacteria: namely, the healthy, scavenging type known as bacilli coli, and the pathogenic or disease-producing kind. In a proper, clean, healthy environment the healthy scavenging bacteria will control the pathogenic kind. When too much fermentation and putrefaction is generated in the colon as a result of neglecting to keep it as free from feces and waste as possible, the pathogenic bacteria proliferate and ailments result.

Sufficient elimination is important no matter how good your diet is.

The very best of diets can be no better than the very worst if the sewage system of the colon is clogged with a collection of waste and corruption. It is impossible, when we eat two, three, or more meals in a day, not to have residue accumulating in the colon in the form of the indigested food particles, as well as the end product from food which has undergone digestion. Furthermore, not only does food waste accumulate in the colon, but also the millions of cells and tissues which have served their purpose and have been replaced. These cells and tissues are dead proteins of a highly toxic nature if allowed to ferment and putrefy, to remain in the colon longer than necessary.

In simple words, the colon is the sewage system of the body. Nature's laws of preservation and hygiene require and insist that this sewage system be cleansed regularly, under penalty of the innumerable ailments, sicknesses and diseases that follow, as the night follows the day, if waste is allowed to accumulate. Not to cleanse the colon is like having the entire garbage collecting staff in your city go on strike for weeks on end! The accumulation of garbage in the streets creates putrid, odoriferous, unhealthy gases which are dispersed in to the atmosphere.

There is no beating around the bush with this man.

SYSTEMATICALLY UNDEREATING

One of my biggest goals in life is regeneration. According to Webster's dictionary "to *regenerate* is to be restored to a better state, refreshed or renewed." In my words, regeneration means becoming younger and living longer. Systematically undereating is a means to regeneration, the key to longevity. Systematic undereating is when you eat just enough food to maintain life while still intaking all the nutrients needed by your body.

The nutritional requirements for each individual vary depending on your level of cellular cleanliness. The person eating a Standard American Diet requires more calories and nutrients to function well. The person eating an all Raw Diet can accomplish the same endurance with less food because when the body is clean, it is more efficient and requires less fuel for energy. Someone who has been on a Raw Diet for 40 years will need less food then someone who has been eating Raw for only five years. And a five year Raw Foodist needs less food then someone eating Raw for one year.

Systematic undereating gives me great results – I never have the heaviness from overeating, my sinuses are clear, I am full of energy, my face glows, and my digestive and elimination systems are flawless. At this point in my journey, my body is traveling at a high speed toward perfection, so when I do not systematically undereat my nose runs and it is obvious I'm not at my optimal level of functioning. After being off track for a few days, I may move into a short fast to build momentum again and refocus.

Especially if you are new to raw foods, stressing out your emotions and body by trying to undereat before you are ready is worse for you then overeating. Systematic undereating is a worthy long-term life goal. Relax, take it slow. All this information is for you to store in your memory and maybe find helpful one day.

LATE NIGHT SNACK

Our most crucial time to regenerate is during sleep. Going to bed on an empty stomach means less work for your body, which equals more time spent on regeneration.

Our eyes have an optic nerve that senses when the sun goes down. As soon as that happens our body goes into dialysis, the cleaning of the kidneys. If our stomachs are full, our body's ability to cleanse and regenerate itself is limited. The Indians instinctively knew this. After sundown, they would not eat again until the next day.

Generally, I never eat after dark. If I need to eat late for some reason, I don't guilt myself. I remember waking up one night with extreme hunger. It was 2 or 3 AM and I got up and juiced some romaine lettuce and carrots. Since it was only liquid, I thought I was safe. I went back to bed and slept soundly. The next day my nose ran nonstop and my eyes were puffy. I recommend not eating late at night.

THE ROLE OF EXERCISE

Exercise is great! However, if you are truly systematically undereating and assimilating all the nutrients your body needs, I believe you can surpass the need for heavy exercise. In other words, if you maintain an optimal intake of food, you could jump up and run ten miles at a moments notice, even if you hadn't run in months. This is the body's natural ability, when given the chance.

When I systematically undereat my body needs barely any food. The little amount of food that you actually *need* to eat could drive you mad. If I run a few miles three or four times a week, my body requires more nourishment. Sometimes I exercise just so I can eat more. If I eat more without exercising, my nose runs and my digestive system is sluggish. When I consume exactly what I need, I'm on top of the world.

My work days are spent at a computer. I don't go outside in the sun or breathe fresh air, and I don't move much. Exercise really helps balance my day. During work I can sit at my computer like a potato and not feel sluggish because I exercised earlier in the day.

The two most important exercises for me are cardiovascular and stretching. When I run, I feel great. I get this natural uplifting high from breathing in massive amounts of fresh air and being out in the sunshine. In addition to running, I love to stretch every muscle in my body and it's been a regular routine of mine for years. To me, stretching is a way to avoid the pains of aging. There have been rare times when I stopped for a few months; but each time, I start to feel like I'm going backwards, my energy isn't as fluid and my muscles get stiff. Then I streeeeeeeetch. Oooooohhhhh yeah! Energy buzzes thru me and I feel loose, young, and agile.

DANGERS IN THE LONG RUN

Since I started the Raw Diet there were times I felt anxious, like I was in a mad dash to become clean. Arnold Ehret's books about fasting inspired me to do numerous kinds of fasts where I tried to eat as little as possible. There were a few two to five day water fasts, and many days when I ate only once. My desire was to move ahead physically, and also spiritually.

The body, when given a chance, always moves toward perfection. During my fasting phase, I may have been listening to my body a bit too much. Following exactly what my body truly needed was moving me closer and closer to

Breatharianism. A Breatharian is someone who does not eat food and lives off the air.

Being this clean can be dangerous. Our body pushes itself to the most ideal state it can reach. The less one eats, the cleaner and tighter their cells become and the more sensitive they are. One is even more vulnerable to air pollution, second hand smoke, processed or cooked food, and so on.

Take air quality for example. Earlier we discussed that air pollution is more dangerous to a cleaner celled raw food eater than a cooked food eater. Going one step further, that same air pollution is more dangerous to a Raw Foodist who eats one small meal a day, compared to a Raw Foodist who eats a lot. When I was eating very little, I had trouble visiting my mom's house in the Valley, a 45 minute drive from Los Angeles. The air pollution was too severe. You'd almost have to live in a bubble if you take cellular tightness too far. The longer you are Raw, the cleaner you become; an extreme diet could limit your lifestyle at some future point.

EAT NUTS

After eating a Raw Diet for many years, you become "locked in" to a certain level of health. Imagine that you have been eating 100% raw food for 40 years. Each year, your body has become cleaner and tighter on a cellular level because your cells have been pouring out toxic endogenous material since you started. Your cells are now so tight and clean that any toxic or impure substance would be more damaging to you than ever before.

The longer you are Raw, the more careful you must be with amounts and quality of foods, concentrated chemicals (intravenous drugs), air pollution, and so on. If you only eat one very small fruit meal each day for 40 years, you will move ahead so fast that living on this planet would become near impossible or at the very least, dangerous. There are too many contaminants and toxins to contend with in our environment and water, not to mention our food supply. Wouldn't it be a shame that in your efforts to become perfectly clean, you actually developed a degenerative disease at an early age due to your vulnerability to the everyday exposure of toxic substances on this planet?

In Hilton Hotema's book there was a story about a man who only ate 12 oz. of food once a day for many, many years. Before this regimen, he was very ill and nothing could be found to cure his sickness except these small meals once a day. Years later, a friend of his challenged him to eat 16 oz. of food. Neither of them thought much of the dare, but after eating those extra 4 oz., the man became grievously ill. He had become "locked in" and any deviation was dangerous. After readopting his previous quantities, the man recovered and continued thriving.

To use another example, a Liquidarian is someone who consumes liquids only. For a five year Liquidarian, the intake of solid food might present a problem. Or what if, after having eaten only one small fruit meal a day for ten years, this man decides to go crazy with all different kinds of raw foods, including nuts. His body, on a cellular level, would be so tight and pure that the new dense food like nuts could cause serious sickness. Fruit is the easiest food for your digestive system. It is practically water. Nuts are much more dense and harder to digest. After ten years of only fruit, nuts can be toxic. If this man wants to eat nuts, he will have to introduce them into his system very slowly, like the snake hunter who intakes the venom, drop by drop.

I feel nuts are an important element in the diet of a Raw

Foodist. Nuts and other dense raw foods, aside from offering nutritious variety, can keep our bodies from moving ahead too quickly.

EATING A GOOD VARIETY OF FOODS

Variety is key to doing well on an all Raw Diet. Many Raw Foodists get into a routine, eating the same meals everyday. I'm guilty. I'll concoct some new salad, and then want to have it night after night. It is not unlike me to eat the same meal for months. Like a drug addiction, my body starts to crave that salad; I look forward to it, and don't want anything else. Luckily, it's not a drug that I am addicted to, it's only vegetables. Nevertheless, if you do not consume enough variety, you cannot manage to consistently give the body all the nutrients it needs, and that will catch up with you in the long run.

Fred's always telling me, "Fine, eat small meals, that's great. Just remember to connect all the dots, be sure you are getting enough variety for nutrients and enough food to maintain." I've finally made it a habit to rotate my dense fatty foods like avocados and different varieties of nuts and raw olives. In addition, I also try to let my fruit meal be determined by what is in season; that way I'm forced into different fruits. More important than all this, however, is my saving grace: juicing. The ideal way to get the widest and largest amount of nutrients is by vegetable juicing.

JUICING

Juicing is extremely important for getting enough nutrients on a Raw Food diet; for "connecting all the dots". When you drink fresh vegetable juice on an empty stomach, the nutrients are easily absorbed and there is no fiber from the food to slow down the process.

Vegetable juice alkalizes your system. We are continually releasing endogenous material from our cells. The juices alkalize this waste, making it much less acidic. It is healthier and easier for the body to handle the release of lower acid poisons. The result is beauty, health, and longevity.

I know an old man that has been juicing religiously for 35 years. He does not have a single gray hair. I'm almost convinced that his dark head of hair is because the poisons that exit his body are alkalized by vegetable juicing; therefore, there are no acidic by-products to turn his hair grey.

Juicing is miraculous, especially when you include a wide variety of vegetables to receive the full spectrum of minerals and other nutrients. Some raw food eaters that I know juice everyday; however, they love the taste of one or two vegetable combinations and never deviate. It's wonderful that they are juicing, but the benefits could be so much greater. I use my favorite tasting vegetables as the base for many of my juices, making sure to add smaller amounts of the many other veggies available.

Dr. Norman Walker experienced the healing power of juice and went on to pioneer the juicing movement. His book, *Fresh Vegetable and Fruit Juices*, studies the different properties of vegetables and outlines the most effective juice combinations for specific organs, general maintenance, and every symptom of dis-ease in the body. I highly recommend adding his book to your collection.

SUPPLEMENTS

Are supplements necessary on a Raw Diet? It depends. If you are starting from a healthy place and are systematically under-eating, juicing, eating a variety of whole foods, and sufficiently eliminating waste, then you may be fine without the daily use of supplements. I feel the best when I am also occasionally including enzymes, probiotics, a super green food, trace minerals, and a B-12 supplement.

Enzymes, when taken with food, aid digestion, and when taken on an empty stomach, speed detoxification. If you are sick, taking enzymes on an empty stomach can be a magic healer. *Probiotics* after a colonic help to support the healthy bacteria in the colon and lessen gas. Probiotics also help bring me back to balance when I am not eating optimally. I rarely take *green food* because I drink two vegetable juices a day; however, green food increases my variety of nutrients and comes to my rescue if I am on the road without a juicer. Products with *minerals* such as brown seaweed extract and alfalfa powder are very important to me, especially after a sauna or good workout. I also take zinc in angstrom absorbable form. *Zinc* is involved in nearly every function and activity of the human anatomy and I don't feel that it is possible to intake the appropriate amount of zinc from my food.

While guzzling delicious vegetable juices and spooning green food supplements, your teeth can easily start to look yellowish and stained. I remember looking in the mirror one day thinking my teeth had rotted; they were such an awful color. Horrified, I assumed my teeth were leaching minerals from the inside out. I refused to go anywhere and couldn't bear to smile. Desperate, I called Dr. Bisci. He explained that my teeth were likely just stained and told me to go to the dentist and get a cleaning; or brush thoroughly with a Sonicare toothbrush while sprinkling on the bristles the supplement Active H. Active H is negatively charged hydrogen ions and is probably the most powerful antioxidant in the United States. Two hours of brushing produced some seriously white teeth. Since then, I learned to rinse my mouth out with water every time I drink a vegetable juice and that helps keep the staining to a minimum. Occasionally, I'll need to use Active H for another teeth whitening treatment. Total cost: 75 cents.

SPIRITUAL REBIRTH

It's been said that once you are 100% Raw and your body becomes cleaner and lighter, reality takes on a more spiritual dimension. One is pushed to consider a more spiritual element to life when they drop the social mainstream ways to travel a path on their own. This was certainly true for me.

My physical body was the first to experience spiritual doors opening. After about six months on raw foods I did the seven day deep tissue cleanse by Bernard Jenson. Since then, I've had an orgasmic like vibration in the center of my forehead. When it first happened, I felt like a wild tiger in the high mountains looking over a cliff into the distance; I felt clear, awake, and alive. What was happening to me? I had no idea, and so, my search began.

I inquired everywhere about the sensation in my forehead. To my dismay, I didn't get many answers. Some people thought that maybe it was marijuana from my college days, detoxifying out of my body. I thought that this might be possible because marijuana stimulates the pineal gland, which is positioned near the front center of the brain. Two years went by, however, and the vibration just got stronger. The marijuana was surely out of my system by then. My search for an answer continued.

Many different cultures talk about energy fields in the body. Chinese tradition calls them meridians or energetic pathways and pressure points. Indian culture identifies with these energy collections in the body as chakras. The chakra located at the forehead is called the Third Eye. Western cultures haven't coined a term for these energy fields, though many scientific studies have definitely proven their existence. Intuitively, I felt that the vibration had something to do with these subtle energies, but couldn't find an answer that made perfect sense to me. Finally, while researching the Raw Food pioneers Dr. Norman Walker and Hilton Hotema, I found what I was looking for.

According to Dr. Norman Walker, in his book The Natural Way to Vibrant Health,

The pineal gland is undoubtedly the spiritual receptacle for life force emanating from the Cosmic Energy of the Universe. The pineal is such a small gland that scientists failed to assign any importance to it until the last 40 years, and even today the strict materialist does not appreciate its mental and spiritual significance.

The mental and spiritual influence of the pineal surpasses that of any other gland. It would almost seem as if this influence is directly connected to the relationship of the physical body of the individual and that mysterious and intangible part known as the soul.

The pineal gland is analogous to a radio antenna, receiving from the atmospheric environment the vital flow of cosmic energy acting like an electric current when it enters the body. Cosmic Energy is that infinite Unfathomable power which permeates the entire universe holding the planets in their course and oper-

ating right into the very core of every atom in your body.

Like the current from one of the huge electric generating sta-tions sending hundreds of thousands of volts through the wires to the 115 volt transformer near your home, so the universal cos-mic energy enters the pineal gland with inexpressibly high volt-age which would virtually burn up the body if the body were not equipped with a transformer to lower that cosmic energy to the voltage consistent with the needs of the individual.

This cosmic energy transformer in the midbrain is known as the thalamus, a structure of a mass of gray cells and tissues in the midbrain which collects the energy from the pineal gland and lowers it and controls it to conform to the physical, mental and spiritual development and needs of the individual. Many people who understand this procedure classify the pineal gland as the spiritual gland in man.

Curiosity took over and I wanted to know more. My ongoing search led me Hilton Hotema who discussed Breatharianism and gifted me with valuable information on the vibrating sensation in my forehead. Hilton Hotema tells that back in ancient times, man was originally Breatharian and had spiritual powers no longer easily accessible in our present state of health. He writes,

The Ancient Masters taught that there is a spiritual realm in man. "The kingdom of God is within you" (Lu. 17:21).

The spiritual realm of god in man is located in the spiritual chambers of the skull, called the golden bowl by the masters (Eccl. 12:6).

These chambers, the function of which is unknown to modern scientists, are five in number. The masters called them the five stars of the microcosm, and they are symbolized in ancient scriptures by certain fives, as the Five Golden Emerods (1 S. 6:4); the Five Loaves (Mat. 14:17), and are known to western science as the five sinus cavities.

The Sankhys Doctrine states that the five physical senses of the conscious man are the exteriorized products of the five corresponding spiritual centers, which are as follows:

Frontal Sinus – A cavity in the frontal bone of the skull.

Sphenoidal Sinus – A cavity in the sphenoid bone of the skull.

Maxillary Sinus – Largest of the five, and resembles a pyramid in shape

Palatine Sinus – A cavity in the orbital process of the palatine bone and opening into either the sphenoidal or a posterior ethmoidal sinus.

Ethmoidal Sinus – This chamber consists of numerous small cavities occupying the labyrinth of the ethmoid bone, and in these cavities are situated the small, mysterious glands known in Occult Science as the Intellectual Organs.

The Sinuses communicate directly or indirectly with the nasal cavity; and it is highly significant to observe that they receive the breath of life directly and unmodified as it flows from the universe to them through the nose, and before any of the other air organs have a chance to select and absorb any substance from the spiritual essence of the cosmos, charged with every known and unknown element.

Due to the degeneration, the Five Spiritual Faculties of civilized man [from eating and breathing polluted air], are dormant, closed, inactive, shut off from receiving the vibratory currents conveying to him the cosmic intelligence of the spiritual world.

The human body was perfectly constituted and designed in the beginning to meet and master all conditions to which it would be subjected in the physical existence on earth.

When man was a breatharian, his body was equipped, in a rudimentary degree, with all parts that would later be needed *[digestive tract], in a functional degree, to prevent him from becoming extinct as a species, regardless of what habits he might adopt or the condition of the environment by which he might be surrounded.*

If you read Hilton Hotema further, you would soon understand that when man was a Breatharian, his digestive tract was dormant and his spiritual organs were in full use. As man started to eat, his dormant digestive tract was called into action, taking energy from his spiritual organs, which soon became dormant. He also says that the closer one becomes to a Breatharian, the more their spiritual organs can reawaken.

Eating Raw is a step closer to the ancient divine man. The digestive track isn't taxed nearly as much, allowing for partial rebirth of the spiritual organs. One thing that most raw food eaters experience is a higher life vibration than before.

Caution: There are dangers involved with Breatharianism and although I am open to anything, I don't believe that in this day and age with our polluted earth, that sustained Breatharianism is possible for most of us.

MEDITATION

I am not going to talk about why meditation is important. Instead, I am going to share some of my experiences. Before becoming Raw at age 25, I had never meditated. The strong vibration in my forehead is what sparked my motivation for spiritual awareness.

Stephen Arlin, in his book *Raw Power*, writes the following:

Meditation is not an obscure Indian method, it is not simply a technique, it is a way of being. Meditation is the greatest adventure the human mind can undertake. It is when you are not doing anything at all. Meditation is not something you can do or practice. It is really just a state in which your mind is completely void of any thought, your body completely void of any movement, and your persona void of any emotion.

This emptying of the mind is wonderful and liberating. It is invigorating and it prepares you to re-enter the world fresh and focused. I have found it to be an essential part of my body building program. One's mind must be clear and focused to perform potentially dangerous feats of strength.

The next sentence he wrote changed my life. *"The best book I've come across on this subject is entitled Meditation: The First and Last Freedom, by Osho."*

Thank you Stephen Arlin! I went to the bookstore to look for my next clue, the book by Osho. They didn't have that particular book, so I purchased a different Osho title. For the first time, I learned how I had been asleep in my ego (asleep in my mind) for all these years and realized I could attain a greater understanding of life through a meditative focus. I read that book practically overnight.

Osho's teaching is meditation. To illustrate his teachings he uses philosophy, shares fun stories, and writes in a way that is very enjoyable to read. Osho's books helped me soar on a spiritual level. I don't consider his teachings a religion, nor do I think of him as my guru. Osho is another powerful inspiration along my journey, as was Dr Norman Walker, Dr. Fred Bisci, and others.

I am an extremist, and the meditation practice I chose to implement was no different. Whether I was walking, running, driving, eating, working, or reading, I was always meditating. Those first few months I barely slept, lying awake in bed from 10 PM to 4 AM trying to meditate. Surprisingly, I felt fairly rested when my morning alarm went off.

My meditative routine looked like this: I became aware of my emotional feelings; the strong ones for me were abandonment, and fear of death. I would then focus on where that pain manifested in my body. For example, if you can imagine any emotion – misery, loneliness, joy – there is always an accompanying physical sensation somewhere in the body. Mostly, my sensations were near my navel area, and I focused there until the pain disappeared. I would do the same for each emotion I felt – fear, greed, love, sadness, happiness – each could be found as a sensation somewhere in the body. From this simple awareness, my understanding of life grew more than I ever could have imagined.

Meditation gifts me with spectacular moments. Every so often, my mind stops chattering and I get a glimpse of life in all its unedited glory. I come out of my mind and can see what is always there in front of me. The world is psychedelic! Everything is connected; the colors, solid matter, sounds, smells, and feelings of life all play together in a symphony of perfection.

Opening the door to a more "in touch" life invited many other fantastic spiritual happenings that don't seem appropriate to share here. I guarantee you'll have your own magic.

SEX ON A RAW DIET

When I was eating cooked food, my libido was through the roof. Any nice looking woman that walked by got me excited. When I became a raw food eater things changed. My sex energy mellowed and matured, and yet it was sparked completely alive again in my next loving relationship. Now, looking at a beautiful woman is like looking at a work of art. On a Raw

Diet, you'll never need to worry about becoming impotent or losing sensation from an over or under stimulated life. You fall into hormonal balance.

Quite a few belief systems around the world preach sexual abstinence for spiritual reasons. In my own research, I read that ejaculating exhausts your energy, which could be used to reach the "ultimate", whatever that is for you. Was that true, and why would sex exhaust energy? Low and behold, Dr. Norman Walker offered yet another answer to one of my many questions. The scientific nature of his reasoning impressed me.

When one considers that the period of reproducing a single orgasm or discharge of the semen requires an average of 35 days, it can readily be appreciated why the excessive discharge of this semen causes weakness, and when deliberately exercised by an adult may cause premature loss of the ability to function sexually. All too often weakness and senility is the result of a lifelong abuse of such a practice.

Twenty percent of the semen is composed of cerebrospinal fluid which is the most vital fluid in the body. The fluid is charged with more Cosmic Energy, or life force, than any other part of the body except the pineal gland and the thalamus. The cerebrospinal fluid flows through the spinal column, fills the eyeballs, lubricates the auditory system and bathes the inner core of every nerve in the body. Every gland in the body is dependent on the cerebrospinal fluid for its sensitive operation, and this includes the hypothalamus.

The spinal fluid is replete with trace elements in greater volume and variety than any other organ in the body. These elements are distributed from the spinal fluid throughout the body by means of the blood and nerves. To appreciate the importance and value of these trace elements you must realize, for example, that many of them are so evanescent that only about 10 or 15 milligrams (a fraction of an ounce of some of them) could be extracted from 2,000 pounds – one ton – of alfalfa, which is one or our riches sources of trace elements.

Because the cerebrospinal fluid emanates from the region of the brain, the unnecessary loss of semen causes weakness and eventual degeneration of the brain cells and tissues. Loss of memory is one of the end-effects of such a disturbance. Man's virility depends upon his conservation of the sperm, not his ability to waste it. Marriage laws and the commandment against adultery were promulgated with this end in view.

Ladies, hide this book from your man! I had always been aware of the exhaustion that followed ejaculation and now I knew why. These days, I only like to ejaculate during very special lovemaking; anything else seems like a waste. *The Multi-Orgasmic Man*, by Montak Chia details exercises and methods about how to orgasm multiple times in one lovemaking session without ejaculating. For women, and men, the book *Peace Between the Sheets* by Marnia Robinson was an eye opener as it convincingly proved how wrong I was to assume that the importance of monitoring orgasmic energy applied only to men. Although I do not condone every word of these two well-meaning books, I do agree with their basic premise and found them good resources for practicing this socially unheard of approach to intimate relationships. Ultimately, for my part, I feel that pleasing a loved one, along with conserving our sperm, is one true responsibility of a man.

CONCLUSION

If you remember one thing from this book, I would want it to be this: *What you leave out of your diet COMPLETELY, with NO CHEATING, is what heals you.* The following list contains the foods from an intermediate diet that Dr. Fred Bisci recommends to many of his clients, whether or not they are transitioning to Raw.

In this book I have stated many of the pros and cons about being a 100% raw food eater. I am not trying to convert you to a completely Raw Diet. Although I feel that it is the optimal diet for the human body if done correctly, it may not be for you. Dr. Bisci's intermediate diet has helped people heal from many degenerative diseases and symptoms of ill health. If you can leave everything out of your diet except these following foods, you will be eating a fabulous diet that will hopefully keep you healthy throughout old age.

INTERMEDIATE HEALING DIET

Raw Fruits

Raw Vegetables

Raw Nuts

Raw Seeds

Sprouts

Steamed Vegetables

Whole Grains (4oz. dry weight) – steamed or cooked in water. Can use basmati brown rice, brown rice, millet, buckwheat, quinoa, or corn meal.

Soy and Rice Milk can be used on grains (White Wave Soy Milk, Westbrae Rice Milk, or Silk Milk (1% or low fat)).

Tinkyada Pasta (wheat and gluten free)

Brown Rice and Beans (2/3 Rice and 1/3 Beans). DO NOT OVEREAT!

Potatoes (3/4 pound) – white, sweet or yam

Wheat and Gluten free bread – 7 Grain Sprouted Bread

is good.

Fish (4-6 oz.) – steamed, broiled or baked (no shell fish)

Chicken (4-6oz.) – steamed, broiled or baked

Turkey (4-6oz.)

SALAD DRESSINGS:

- Flaxseed oil or extra virgin olive oil with fresh lemon or raw apple cider vinegar.
- Annie's or Walden Farms no fat dressings are acceptable in some cases (no egg yolks or milk solids).
- Braggs Amino Acids

IMPORTANT NOTE: Do not eat starch and animal protein in the same meal

IMPORTANT NOTE: Do not eat animal protein more than three times a week

IMPORTANT NOTE: Drink fresh green vegetable juices everyday

If you only eat these foods, without cheating, you are on your way to excellent health. If and when you are able to take your diet to the next level, I recommend that you first eliminate all starches on this list. And you can just keep going from there!

Colonics are very beneficial especially when improving your diet.

MY DIET

My diet and lifestyle have come a long way over the last five years. I run 2 1/2 miles, three or four times a week. These are the only days that I consider drinking a good amount of fruit juice. After heavy exercise, the body stops producing insulin for about

45 minutes, making this window the ideal time for fruit juice. Fresh squeezed orange juice is my favorite and I drink an 8 to 12 oz. glass after my run. Once that digests, I have a green drink with carrot juice in it. On the days I don't run, I drink the juice of one orange to get vitamin C for my connective tissue.

Between 11:30 AM and 2 PM I have my first meal, Apple Flax. I blend about three Fuji apples and mix in three tablespoons of ground golden flax seeds. If I don't eat that, a mono-meal of seasonal fruit is enough to satisfy me. Later in the day, I drink another green vegetable juice.

Dinner is between 3 and 6 PM, and is usually a salad. My current favorite is as follows: Half a large head of romaine lettuce, chopped. I throw in small amounts of any vegetables that looked good at the market. To that I add one handful of sugar snap peas and 3-6 olives, chopped. A nice amount of sprouts and half a squeezed lemon, and I'm just about done. Choosing one large avocado, I scoop out the insides and put it in the bowl with the rest of the ingredients. Then I knead the entire mixture by hand, mashing the avocado into the salad as it mixes with the lemon. Lastly, I cut up about four tomatoes and throw those in, too. Delicious.

Sometimes, I'll eat a few nuts before my salad meal. If eating nuts, I use fewer olives or eliminate them completely to avoid too many different fats at once. Variations of salads are endless. Play, and let the seasons guide your ingredients.

PHOTOS

BEFORE RAW

8 MONTHS RAW

4 1/2 YEARS RAW

DR. FRED BISCI

AN INTERVIEW WITH DR. FRED BISCI

Part of my job Monday thru Friday is talking with people about nutrition. I have come to Dr. Bisci with hundreds of questions from people around the globe. There has never been a question he could not answer, in detail. Regardless of whether people's concerns are about arthritis and Crohn's disease or indigestion and migraines, he always has an answer, a solution. In every case he knows what foods should be added or eliminated and what supplements are needed to speed recovery. I have seen it happen time and time again that Fred's nutritional advice has empowered people to heal from degenerative diseases of all kinds.

Sometimes he and I also talk about more personal questions concerning life, relationships, exercise, and spiritual and personal growth. His advice always hits my heart. Fred is like a father to me. While reading his interview, you will soon realize that a good amount of information in Raw Spirit was inspired by this man. Dr. Bisci has a PhD in Nutrition, and has seen well over 25,000 people during his 50 year career. In addition, Fred has been Raw for over four decades. He has a "super brain" that works like a computer and a purity of character that inspires me. We are fortunate Fred has agreed to participate in this interview. Thank you Fred for taking the time.

Not many people understand what happens to their body on a cellular level when they improve their diet. Do you feel that understanding this concept would result in much better health amongst the Raw Food community?
Definitely! Yes, it's very important to understand that the human body is made up of trillions of different cells and that

all diseases begin on a cellular level. Renal failure of the kidneys, colon cancer, lung cancer, heart disease, osteoporosis...Our genetic makeup and quality of lifestyle determine *when* and *where* our bodies start to break down into eventual disease. If you keep the body clean on a cellular level the chance of you getting sick is much slimmer. If it is going to happen based on genetics, then it will happen at a much later stage in life.

It really is imperative that a person understands how cellular change happens so they can appreciate the importance of keeping their body clean and can better formulate a program to do just that. A program to cleanse the body should be based on what harmful foods are left out of one's diet *completely* such as refined sugar, processed starches, and animal protein. We also need to make sure we get all the nutrients – vitamins, minerals, proteins, carbohydrates, and so on – that we need for the body to function as an efficient biological machine.

Can you talk a little about how someone can become cleaner on a cellular level?
The basic way that a person becomes cleaner on a cellular level, is very simple. Follow the concept that what you *leave out* of your diet is critically important. How we intoxicate ourselves on a cellular level is based on our lifestyle. A simplistic solution would be to stop indulging in those things that are causing us problems and leading to toxemia on a cellular level. If you leave out everything that interferes with a healthy physiology and give the body a chance to revitalize itself on a cellular level, you have a very good chance at becoming a much healthier person. You are at less risk of developing a degenerative disease, and if you are already afflicted with a chronic condition, the body's God given reme-

dial capabilities can assist you. I believe almost any disease can be overcome, when given the chance.

There are other ways to cleanse the body in a therapeutic manner. For instance, certain cleanses can target specific organs, such as your liver and colon. There are also different forms of exercises frequently used in other cultures that are actually very vitalizing on a cellular level.

Why is it bad to go back and forth from a Raw Food Diet to a cooked food diet?
That can be a disaster because it takes time for a body to accommodate what you are putting into your system. It takes the average person a lifetime to gradually introduce some of the negative things in their dietary lifestyle. For example, if a person were to take a tablespoon of arsenic all at once it would probably kill them. Let's say they took one drop every third day and gradually every week increased it. In the matter of a year or two they could probably take 2 or 3 tablespoons and it might not affect them. It is the same with your diet. Ever since you were young, you have gradually continued eating and living a lifestyle that is not conducive to a healthy physiology. Let's say all of a sudden you clean your body up, which on a very clean diet would only take a matter of months or a year. Then one day you have a weak moment and binge with foods that previously took you a lifetime to work up to. Your body won't be able to tolerate it because you did not give it enough time to accommodate what you are doing. The impact could be 100 times more disastrous then if you had gone back gradually.

Why is it necessary to leave something out of our diet *completely* if we want to heal? Why can't we cheat just a little bit every once in a while?

The answer to that is for the reason that I just explained. Leaving things out of your diet is critically important, and without omitting them completely, your body will never respond to what you are doing. If I was eating a perfect diet and I was smoking crack once every two weeks, my body would never cleanse itself. That is an exaggerated analogy of what is really happening. Everything is chemical and everything is action and reaction. If you leave something out completely, the body will progress to another level. It will not go to that other level unless you give it the freedom to go.

Many people think they're feeling good and doing well. They don't realize that their habits are nowhere near optimal and that they are far from experiencing their full potential of health. Unfortunately, they will have to answer for it later on in life with some kind of degenerative disease. Even if the degenerative disease doesn't kill them, it may likely leave them incapacitated.

What is the order of food groups that one should leave out of their diet from first to last?
If you are talking from a moral or spiritual standpoint, of course we should be leaving out the animal protein because all life is sacred, not to mention the fact that commercial animal protein uses up more of our earth's resources compared to other food groups. Yogurt and dairy products are from animals; however, there is no killing involved, so from a spiritual perspective that can be seen as acceptable.

From a physical standpoint, it is very questionable what is really more harmful. Is it the refined sugar, the processed carbohydrates, or the animal protein? They all have consequences. If a person is eating these foods, but also has in their diet a good amount of fruits and vegetables, is drinking enough water, and is drinking vegetable juices, they will be better off. These latter foods are like an antidote for the poison. If eaten before, they compensate for some of the ill effects. The ideal thing for a cooked a food eater is to eat a plant based diet and moderate amounts of the other foods. Of course we know that if a person can eat an all raw diet, that is optimal. A raw food eater has to make sure they are getting everything they need. Some raw food eaters run into marginal deficiencies in the long run. They would do better if they saw raw food eating as a science, rather than a philosophy.

I mention in this book that a raw food eater is more sensitive to polluted air than a cooked food eater. Do you feel your health is suffering because you are a Raw Foodist living in NY air pollution?

Of course it is not the optimal environment, but the body has about a 20% margin of error and we are able handle certain things. Not everyone can live in a pristine environment. We have a life to lead. I know a lot of people that retreat to Costa Rica, Ecuador, or some of these other places. They try to live Garden of Eden like lives in the jungle, just living on fruit. Most people I have seen didn't do well at all. I know people that actually died from trying. I know one person that was paralyzed for awhile. They got very sick with parasites living mostly on a fruitarian diet. Johnny Lovewisdom thought he was going to do that. He moved to Ecuador and died a horrible death. I have seen plenty of people try to do these types of things, thinking they were getting cleaner and cleaner. In my opinion, they didn't really understand the underlying workings of the body, especially as far as blood gases are concerned, which I really don't want to go into here.

Why do you think Dr. Norman Walker lived to be such

an old age?

Based on the concept of what you leave out of your diet completely; he definitely understood that. Everyone might not agree with his diet, but the juices are dynamic. The juices are a very powerful alkalizer. They erase our mistakes. Many people into raw foods believe that juices are a fractured food. I believe they are seriously mistaken. Juicing just takes the place of your teeth. Be sure not to overdo anything and balance any fruit juices with vegetable juice to help stabilize the absorption of sugars.

I think Norman Walker was way ahead of his time. There are people today that still criticize him, yet I think they are sadly mistaken. Plus, take a look at his lifespan. Even though he didn't eat a 100% raw food diet, I don't know of many people who lived as long as he did. Healing diets must be done correctly because even those eating all raw are definitely not living any longer then anybody else and there has to be a reason for that.

What kinds of problems can someone run into who eats too much fruit?

What I do is look at the situation anecdotally. Personally in the last 40 years, I haven't seen any Fruitarian, someone that ate 100% fruit or even close to it, that did well over a long period of time. I love fruit. Years ago I ate a lot of fruit while doing a lot of long distance running. I suffered some consequences.

When you are eating too much sugar, no matter where it comes from, you are suffering from Hyperinsulin. It is not a good idea to have a lot of insulin floating around in your blood even though you will have tremendous amounts of energy. In addition, the ratio of sugar to minerals definitely causes a problem. If you add up the nutrients and the calories, the balance between the sugar and other nutrients, excess fruit is certainly not ideal. There are some people that eat a diet of a lot of fruit and they compensate through exercise. If you want to stabilize your sugar by exercising 3 or 4 times a day, you might be able to do that, but you can run into problems on a nutrient level. I have met plenty of Fruitarians and as soon as you start speaking to them, you can sense their high level of irritability. I believe it might have a lot to do with a B12 deficiency, which you can run into, although that's not always the case. To me, a lot of fruit in one's diet is definitely not the optimal way to go.

How much fruit is too much?

Well that depends on the person. I don't think that one size fits all. We are all biochemically different individuals. There are some people who can eat more fruit than others and still be ok. I would gage the amount of fruit we eat based on our activity. If you are a marathon runner, of course you can eat more fruit then the person that is sedentary.

When you eat the right type of diet I find that you don't need as much exercise as people think you need. If you are eating a right diet and your body is clean on a cellular level you will have great endurance anyway. I have done it myself. I have laid off exercise for years and was able to go out and run 10 miles with no problem. I believe that your body is a biochemical efficient biological machine and you don't have to fine-tune it by training to increase your oxygen uptake.

You have mentioned that long term raw food eaters can run into problems if given pharmaceutical or intravenous drugs. Why is this?

Your body chemistry has the ability to accommodate just about anything. Like the example before, if you gave a person a large amount of arsenic it would kill them. If you took a very small amount, maybe one drop at a time, over a long period of time, and you gradually increase it, the body chemistry can accommodate a lot more then if it was given all at once. Again, it is the same thing with food. As your body adjusts to eating a cleaner diet, it adapts itself to a much cleaner level. If you were to give a person that has been on a 100% raw food diet pharmaceuticals or intravenous drugs, the body does not have enough time to gradually accommodate to where it can tolerate a concentrated chemical. It is a risky situation and there are a thousand variables in this type of a thing, which I plan on elaborating sometime later on.

You have been on a raw diet for over four decades. Have you ever encountered a problem with medical drugs?
Absolutely. It has happened to me a few times. That is why I became so aware of how it can be potentially dangerous. Now, it doesn't mean that it's definitely going to happen to everybody, because as I said before there are a thousand variables in the human chemistry. If someone has really been on an all raw diet, the chances of this are much higher. Many people say that they are on an all raw diet and the diet could be 60% or 70% raw. This type of person is at much less of a risk than the person that has been on a 100% raw diet.

About 30 years ago I went to a dentist and I let him convince me to use nitrous oxide. My body's reaction was so severe that if I got any sicker, I could have had a heart attack. My heart was pounding; I thought it was going to break through my chest. I couldn't make the dentist aware that I was having problems because I was being put to sleep. Fortunately, I was able to get my left hand up in the air and he took the mask off of me. I have had other experiences in my earlier years where

I tried taking some things to see the effect it would have on me. The results were much more profound then I expected. I am not saying that everyone would have this experience but I am well aware of what can happen to me, and I assume that other people could have similar reactions.

Do you feel that raw food eaters should be raising their newborn babies Raw?

Part of the problem is that there are a lot of people that are getting incorrect information on how to raise their baby on raw foods. In addition, when that child goes to school, if he or she is not home schooled, he or she is going to be subjected to pccr prcoourc. I havo ooen children that were raised Raw and then put into public schools. They were switching food with other children and eating whatever was provided in the cafeterias. They had many problems and they got sick.

There are a lot of complications. Parents should be fully aware of what they are doing. They should be prepared to home school their children, they should know what all the social ramifications are down the road, and they should know what can happen as far as the legalities of not having medical supervision, and so on. If that is what they want to do, then I am perfectly comfortable with it. I have had two incidences here in NY where the people had their children taken from them. There are a lot of things to consider and I am very concerned when people tell me they want to raise their children Raw. Still, there is no doubt in my mind that a raw food diet is the best way to go as long as it is done correctly.

I don't know anyone that is a bigger animal lover then you. How do you recommend someone raise his or her pet?

It is best to get as close as you can get to their natural adaptation. I knew a guy that had two dogs and he wanted to bring them up on a vegetarian diet. The dogs did not do well. The dogs were always very thin, had a tremendous appetite, and they were outside eating dirt and wood all the time.

On the other hand, raising a dog on a Raw Diet is fantastic. I did it myself. I gave my dog raw meat of course. She had cardiomiopothy at a very young age and she wouldn't have lived long. I am positive I prolonged her life at least 6 years. She did get sick later on, again with cardiomyopothy. I had to take her to a vet and when he medicated her, she actually died within 24 hours because it was her first medication.

Do the best you can with your pet's diet. I have two English Mastiff's now. What I do with those dogs is supplement their diet. I give them some pet food and I supplement it with raw food. I put raw eggs in their meals, green food, and flax seed oil. Some people are purists and don't believe in supplements for animal or humans. Insufficient supplementation is one of the reasons why a lot of individuals have failed. They didn't have a full understanding and they didn't take everything into consideration. I think it is very simplistic to think what a person or what an animal would do in uncivilized nature is the ideal. Also, one must take into consideration how toxic they are and what the endogenous material can do coming out of their systems.

How do you feel about the use of alcohol?
I don't believe in drinking alcohol. Even though there are people that say a very small amount of alcohol is therapeutic, I don't believe that. I believe that what you leave out of your diet is critically important. We have to eat the best diet possible and be fully aware of what may happen.

The better the diet, the more release of endogenous material. We have to understand what the release of endogenous material can do to a person. I believe that is why a lot of people on raw foods have failed in the long run. In my observation in the last 40 years, people on raw foods are not really living any longer then other people. I know plenty of people right now in their 80's, 90's, and close to a hundred whose diets are not that great. People like us that are eating raw diets should be exceeding that as far as I am concerned. I believe there are many factors, which I'm sure I'll target in this interview, that haven't been addressed by most Raw Foodists.

How do you feel about the use of marijuana?
I am against it. I don't believe in the use of anything that is going to alter your chemistry. Just because it is a plant and you are going to eat it or smoke it doesn't mean that it's good, even though it makes you feel good. I am against the use of anything that has a pharmicalogical effect on your body or your brain. I know there are a lot of people in the raw food community that do things like that. I am totally against it.

Do you feel that colonics are important?
Yes. Many people, myself included, thought that colonics and enemas were totally unnatural. I have learned from my mistakes. I have seen cases where enemas and colonics have made a huge difference between someone living or dying. It might not be natural but sometimes it is therapeutically expedient in helping them release the endogenous material still inside their system.

Of course there are going to be people that disagree with me. I have to question how much experience they really have with what colonics and enemas can do. My experience shows me that colonics done intelligently at the right time can be very beneficial for a person that needs them.

For example, I have seen people into raw foods who, after

awhile, weren't doing well and tried fasting as a remedy. Fasting is not a panacea and it doesn't work all the time. They ended up running into trouble because they were already in a serious healing crisis from their raw diet and all they did was add another crisis creating situation – fasting. Therefore, the crisis got even more severe. Colonics would have been a better way to go.

Also, I know a natural hygienist that developed colon cancer. I'm unsure of the exact circumstances around his situation, but to my understanding, he went on a fast to cure his cancer but didn't get better; he got worse. He got so disillusioned with what was happening that he went for chemotherapy, and died after a few weeks in treatment. If colonics had been a part of his treatment or better yet, a part of his lifestyle before he developed cancer, he would likely have had different results.

Do you feel that one needs to do colonics to be successful on a raw food diet?
Not necessarily. I don't feel colonics are an absolute necessity. There are plenty of people that don't have to do colonics. Although they could benefit from them, colonics are not always absolutely necessary. I know plenty of natural hygienists who refuse colonics and still do well.

I have talked to you about how I have had gas and waste problems ever since I became Raw. Is this normal?
Well it's not normal, but it can happen. There are people I call colonic bulimics. In other words, if you are frequently overeating or binging and use a colonic to make up for these unfavorable habits, then it is definitely not the right way to go, and you'll still have excess gas and waste. A person like this might need a fast to rebalance their chemistry. This is where

the natural hygiene concepts can really come into play.

Part of the problem, of course, is that people are medicating themselves with food and not able to deal with the real issues at hand. Digestive discomfort may also surface if you are going through an emotional or psychological detox, which is just like food. You could also be eating too late at night. There are all kinds of things that you could be doing.

Even when I am eating really well, feeling emotionally okay, and have been eliminating fine, inevitably after two weeks, gas and waste build up in my system and I need to do a colonic.

That is possible. These are not simple issues. You see, it takes years for people to really balance out. There are other factors as well. We are aliens in our own environment. You can actually get to the point where you are so clean that the environment, the very air, can be causing you minor symptoms of illness. There are over 10,000 chemicals in our environment. They are in our carpets, in our clothes, and all around us.

Years ago I took my diet to the limit and was so clean that the environment was making me very uncomfortable. I had to back down from what I was doing. This made me aware of certain things concerning raw foods that people just do not understand. It is not just about making your diet 100% raw. You have to take into consideration that your body may not be able to handle the elimination of what you have stored over a lifetime. You may even have to consider genetics, the diet and lifestyle of your mother and grandmother.

We all know the right things to do for our body. But do we know what happens to us as a result of doing the right thing? Can our body handle what's being released into the blood based on that change? That is where all the mistakes have been made. That is the reason why Norman Walker lived to be 118 and no other natural hygienist or fruitarian lived to be 90 or 100. Dr. Esser was a brilliant guy. What happened to Dr. Esser? He died when he was 92, which is fantastic. But if our diet and knowledge is so great, why aren't we living beyond what other people are living? Norman Walker lived longer than anybody I know. He wasn't a raw food eater. He ate some cooked food, but was also heavy into juicing and colonics. I think that should speak for itself.

I do colonics a couple times per month. Is it bad to do it this many times?

It is an individual thing, Matt. The whole problem is that everyone is looking for a response that one size fits all. That is part of the problem with some of the people into raw foods. There are a thousand variables in the human chemistry. The same thing doesn't work for everybody. I know we are all human beings and that the basic approach to live on a raw diet could probably be taught in 10 minutes, but many details of a raw diet are controversial.

I have been into raw foods in one degree or another for almost 50 years. The same basic controversy exists right now as it did years ago. People are still arguing about fruit, fats, enemas, juice fasting versus water fasting, and they say it like their one thing is a panacea. Look back at everyone who has followed a raw diet. Where are the leaders in this movement? How long did they live? What did they die from? Why have so many circum to cancer? There has got to be a reason why raw food eaters aren't living beyond what other people are living.

Is it possible to do too many colonics?

It can definitely become a problem. Anything can be overdone. You can even drink too much water. I knew a guy once that had an obsession with drinking water. He needed to go in for some routine tests at a hospital. To ensure good results, he thought it would be good to drink a lot of water beforehand. A couple gallons later, he passed out. The people in the emergency room thought he had a stroke. The doctor diagnosed it as water intoxicosis – too much water. Insane, but true.

Anything can be too much. You can eat too much, even good foods. You can hyperventilate by taking in too much air. I know some people from the US that went to South America, became Fruitarians and died. They couldn't handle the sudden transition from a toxic environment to a very clean location and lifestyle. The release of endogenous material is what killed them. There was nothing wrong with what they were doing. It was just too much of a change from one extreme to another. They went from a bad environment to a very good environment, and a bad diet to a very good diet. Maybe if they did colonics down there it wouldn't have happened to them.

How do you feel about Bernard Jensen's psyllium and bentonite cleanse?

While I know some people who are against these types of cleanses, I also know many who have benefited from them. If someone is detoxifying too rapidly, there are things, such as Bernard Jensen's cleanse, that you can do to help unburden the liver. I am not against it at all. You can sometimes do this cleanse without having to put a person on an extreme fast.

Again, one size does not fit all. The person doing the cleansing should have someone competent helping them. In some cases support might not be called for, and for others it could be very beneficial.

Bernard Jenson did succumb to cancer. They actually said that he had cancer, then got better, and then died in an accident. I don't know what really happened. He was 92 years old so he did some things right. The bottom line to me is how healthy they are and how long they live.

After I did the psyllium bentonite cleanse I started to experience the energy fields that I mention in this book for the first time. Can you comment on that?
Once again, one size does not fit all. Everybody is different. Anecdotal information is not something that should be read too much into. If someone tells you about his or her experience, that doesn't mean that it is inevitable for you. A better sign is how it works in general with many people that have tried similar things.

How do you feel about the aluminum content in bentonite clay, one of the major ingredients of Bernard Jensen's cleanse?
I know some people that don't recommend bentonite because they think it has aluminum in it. Bentonite contains montemarilionite, which is different. It is not being absorbed into your system.

Do you think this Bernard Jensen's cleanse would drastically improve someone's health and level of cleanliness?
It all depends upon who the person is and what the circumstances are in a situation.

When I was eating cooked foods, I ate everything and anything and never had any noticeable digestive problems. Why, now that I'm Raw, must I contend with annoying digestive upsets (gas) whenever I eat bad food combinations?
When you eat raw foods, proper food combining makes a big difference because the enzymes are intact. The other reason

is, as you get healthier the body responds more loudly to mistakes. Bodies eating a lot of cooked food, do not have the vitality to respond with quick force.

After you have been eating Raw a long time, combining foods won't have as much of a harsh effect on you. I don't always have to combine my foods well and I still feel good. However, I do notice a little bit of gas and less endurance. Where it really makes a difference is during a run. Especially at my age, if I am eating right combinations, and go out for a run, I can definitely run further. In other words, I have more energy because I expended less energy breaking down and utilizing my food.

Good food combining does make you more efficient as far your level of energy. You will also have better absorption and less gas. There are plenty of people that don't combine their foods and seem to be okay. When you are first getting into a Raw Diet, food combining does make a difference. However, you could have gas anyways because on this diet the body releases a large amount of endogenous material that needs to be eliminated. That is where enzymes and probiotics can help.

Some people say that you shouldn't mix too many types of fats at one meal. How do you feel about that?
The more you mix your foods, the greater burden you put on your digestive system. The simpler your diet, the more effective you are going to be. Keep in mind, however, that the simpler your diet is, the faster your body responds, and it kind of "locks" you in at that level.

Everything is chemical and everything is action and reaction. That is why when people eat a lot of fruit or stick to a fruitarian diet and then try to eat nuts, they can't handle them. It doesn't mean nuts are bad. It means the body's ability to digest concentrated foods has been lost because they haven't been using it. Your body's chemistry always responds to what you are doing or not doing. To eat nuts again, you would have to take the time to gradually reintroduce them so your body could accommodate the addition of a new dense food. Some people call this the law of accommodation.

In regards to mixing fats, do the best you can. It is all a question of evolving to be better and better as time goes on. When you get to a point where you are not wrapped so tight, when the emotional and psychological impact is not so intense, you can go to the next level. So if you are going to mix a few olives with an avocado once in awhile, you don't want to feel guilty over doing something like that. It certainly is not going to kill you especially if you are doing everything else right. If you belch a couple times the next day, it isn't the end of the world. Some of the people into raw foods get a bit neurotic and that attitude can be contagious.

What are your thoughts on Hyperbaric Medicine?
I believe in hyperbaric medicine. We have to realize that a hyperbaric chamber (hyperbaria) and hyperbaric oxygen chamber are two different things. If you are using a hyperbaric oxygen chamber (hyperoxia) with 100% pure oxygen under a lot of pressure, it can pose a potential problem. Conversely, a hyperbaric chamber uses ambient air and moderate amounts of pressure. Under a doctor's supervision, you can add a small amount of oxygen. It is critically important to know the difference between these two chambers.

A lot of people into the natural thing are totally against hyperbaric chambers because they believe that only nature can and should create the perfect balance of oxygen in your blood. Granted, if our blood was perfect and everything in life was perfect, more oxygen would be counter indicated. Yet I have seen oxygen therapy do wonders for people. A man in a coma-induced stroke was put into a hyperbaric chamber. With my own eyes I witnessed this man come out of a coma. Would anything else have triggered results like this? What could you have done, put him on a fast? Of course not; you couldn't do it. Did he come out of his coma? Yes he did. Am I going to say that one size fits all and added oxygen is never good? That is ridiculous.

I have been in a hyperbaric chamber myself and seen the benefits of it. In my lifetime I have had a few injuries. At one point I was what you might call a kind of adventurer. I've taken some chances and had some accidents. I saw how much faster I recovered in a hyperbaric chamber while on a raw diet.

In last year's Super Bowl there was a tight end for the Philadelphia Eagles and he had broken his ankle. The doctors said it would take many months for him to recover. A month later he was back playing in the Super Bowl. When asked about his speedy recovery, he said he had spent a lot of time in a hyperbaric chamber. Each case is individual. Supervision is imperative when using hyperbaric methods.

Why do you feel that raw food eaters seem to be dying at the same age as cooked food eaters?
That takes a lot of explanation. If a person is coming from a very toxic lifestyle and they begin a 100% raw food diet, they need to understand about the release of endogenous material. They need to keep ahead of the endogenous material coming out of them; otherwise, the buildup of endogenous material in addition to our daily exposure to exogenous toxins, can shorten life.

The long-term raw food eater must continue methods of deep cleansing, such as colonics and infrared sauna, because as time goes on, they become tighter and cleaner on a cellular level and naturally more sensitive. At this stage of cleanliness, the daily exposure to exogenous toxins, the greatest of these being our polluted environment, has a more serious impact on them. That is the reason why even though they are much better off in the beginning, the gap between when a raw food eater dies and when a cooked food eater dies is so narrow. Those who take steps to stay ahead of the intoxication from our environment and their own cellular detoxification, seem to be living the longest and doing the best.

Why are those that have been eating a raw diet for many decades at more risk of running into serious complications compared to others?
It is for the very same reason that I ran into trouble during the nitrous oxide episode at the dentist years ago. My body was so clean that the nitrous oxide was poisonous. As if I had ingested poison, my heart started to beat rapidly and my body was trying to get it out of my system as fast as it possibly could. The cleaner you are, the less ability you have to tolerate negative things without a reaction. If something is really bad, your reaction can be disastrous.

A few years back I started feeling really sick. I turned to fasting to try and heal. 38 days later, I was not feeling any better. Knowing I needed to try something else, I began a regimen of enzymes and probiotics. Lucky I did, otherwise, I wouldn't be here. Some people said that I just didn't fast long enough. That is ridiculous.

Why are eating nuts so important for a raw food eater in the long run?

Can a person survive on a very sparse diet or on only one specific food? Yes they can survive, but the body requires certain nutrients to thrive. You can exist without nuts, but why risk not getting enough protein and fatty acids. Nuts are important. You don't need a lot of them. A moderate amount of nuts complements a raw food diet. There are people who don't eat the nuts and seem to be doing okay. However, it is very questionable how they will do in the long run. I went years without eating nuts and some of the effects, although subtle, were not optimal.

I recommend that a person on a raw food diet eat fruits, vegetables, nuts, and seeds in the proper balance, without overdoing anything. I think part of the problem is that some people want to eat a tremendous amount of one type of food such as fruit or nuts and don't pay too much attention to the other raw foods.

There are things you need to take into consideration such as climate. In a colder climate you need concentrated foods to keep you warm, so it may be good to eat more nuts. Sometimes one person might need a little more fat or protein in their diet. It is possible to exist on only fruits and vegetables if you also eat super green food and sprouts. But again, it is not one size fits all. I always like to know what a person is doing before I tell them what they really need. For example, if a person is eating a lot of sprouts they might not need the nuts.

If you are eating fruit, nuts help stabilize your blood sugar. I like to see people eat fruit with a little celery or romaine lettuce, wait 45 minutes, and then have a small handful of nuts. Otherwise, if you are eating a lot of fruit, but not eating nuts, your blood sugar is bouncing up and down. That is one of the reasons a lot of people binge on fruit.

When I was up at the raw food expo, I was watching people eat fruit from 7:00 in the morning to 11:00 at night. Every time I saw them, they were eating watermelon, mangos, grapes, or some other fruit. It was bizarre to me. And all the while someone there was convincing them it was okay to do! I don't think that it is okay, not at all.

You also need concentrated foods to hold the water in your body so you don't urinate too much. Sometimes if I don't eat any nuts, I urinate a lot. You can lose minerals doing that.

You have been on a Raw Diet for 40 years. It would be very hard for you to go back to eating foods that are not raw. If you could do it all over again, would you add any other foods into your diet?

I would never consider going back, because if I did go back I know what would happen. In the early years I tried experimenting with things like that. The impact was so bad it was unbelievable.

When I first got into raw foods, I was kind of naïve because I took everybody at their word. There were a lot of people pushing a 100% raw food diet. Later I found out that not only were they not on it themselves, but that years later they turned against it. They changed their mind completely about raw foods because they did not do well on it. I respect what everybody says but I don't take it as gospel truth. I know plenty of people right now who are saying things that I know are just not true. I agree that it is possible to be healthy without following a 100% raw food diet, but those making the claims against raw foods are not speaking from enough experience, and that's what bothers me.

How about adding raw goat's milk or raw cheese to your diet?

I am Italian; cheese was a big thing when I was a kid. If I thought I could eat raw goat's cheese, I definitely would. The only problem is that years ago, every time I tried eating it, my throat would get sore and I felt sick. Plenty of Raw Foodists I know do well eating raw goat milk and goat cheese.

How old do you think someone could live in this day and age if they committed to an optimal Raw Diet?
There are many variables. Emotional and psychological well being has a lot to do with your health in general. Also, the environment you are living in; whether it is a tropical climate with clean air, or not. How much stress you are under is another big factor.

My lifestyle is very stressful. I work with a lot of people all day long and still make mistakes in my diet. I don't get nearly enough rest; I don't sleep. You might be able to classify me as an over-achiever or maybe a workaholic. I can't believe I sleep enough, even though I function well. With only three of four hours sleep, I get up the next morning and run at the same pace I did the day before. Am I getting enough rest? Probably not. Is the stress in my life becoming unhealthy? Yes, it probably is. Eventually I am going to have to answer for my choices. I am aware of that. For 75 years old, I'm functioning very well. Am I doing as well as I could be? No. Probably not.

If everything was perfect, I think we could live a very long time. I won't put a number on it. Norman walker lived to be 112 or 118. He too could have probably done better. If he were here now, I bet he would have agreed.

Living longer also requires cleansing your body on a cellular level. I think that is a very important issue. Sometimes you can't do it with a Raw Diet alone. That is where fasting comes into play. My belief about when people should be fasting is different than most. Starting a fast when I feel at my best is when I get the greatest results. When you are in a crisis, you can sometimes use fasting to heal. But fasting is a crisis-creating situation in itself. If you want to really go deeper into tissue cleansing, the opportune time to fast is when you are at your best. That is where fasting becomes anti-aging. If you fast during a crisis, it's really not anti-aging; I am definitely going to write a book about that.

Do you feel that eating once a day is a big key for longevity? Eating once a day, if done correctly, can have amazing results. However, I think you can live a long life without eating just once a day. If you eat a low calorie, nutrient dense diet once a day, you have to make sure you are still getting all the nutrients you need. If you didn't eat the right food, it could be a disaster.

What we must be careful of as we age, and especially on a raw food diet, is to not run into any marginal deficiencies, which can so easily go undetected. I just had a case the day before yesterday where someone had been on a raw diet for about five years and he wasn't feeling well at all. He was vitamin B-12 deficient. He had every symptom. After taking vitamin B-12 a few days, he noticed a difference. It's possible you may not need a B-12 supplement, but I usually recommend it for most people.

You can easily slip into marginal deficiencies and not know it. If you are pumping yourself up with sugar, you won't recognize marginal deficiencies because of all the sugar floating around in your blood. Without knowing it, you are probably suffering from hyperinsulin.

The key is to eat a variety of foods to make sure you get enough of everything. If you can do that in one meal, fine. You will be better off and you are going to have much more energy. Anybody that tries eating one meal a day, will feel a big increase in their energy levels after four or five one meal days. However, if you are a marathon runner, you might not be able to get enough energy, nutrients, and calories in one meal to satisfy your body's needs. Every case is individual and one size does not fit all. Nobody really has to run marathons to be healthy. In some respects it might not be that good for you because of free radical damage. I have run many marathons. Now looking back on my life, I think that a lot of that just has to do with your ego or proving something to yourself. When you are eating a really good diet, it isn't necessary to exercise extensively for health. You are better off exercising moderately everyday, getting fresh air, sunshine, doing some resistance and aerobic exercises and some form of stretching. This way, you won't need to eat a tremendous amount of calories to sustain yourself. Whenever you are eating a tremendous amount of calories to sustain a high level of exercise, you are not really doing what is optimal for your health.

Do you feel that systematically under eating is a big key in longevity?
That has a lot to do with what I just said. A big problem with everybody in general is that food is really an addiction. A lot of the overeating that people do is primarily to medicate themselves with food. When a person gives up eating a bad diet, in most cases they still have that addiction with food emotionally and psychologically. You don't get rid of that just by eating a better diet.

There is a lot to systematical under eating. You can under eat and not be nourished. You need to make sure you are getting everything you need based on your activity level and you need to be emotionally and psychologically stable enough to reap the full benefits.

Do you feel that exercise is key to longevity?
Exercise is a very important part of the equation just like diet, fresh air, sunshine, emotional psychological stability, and adequate rest. A person that is really clean and healthy does not have to exercise very hard to maintain that part of the equation. They don't have to do a lot. They could exercise for 20 minutes to a half hour a day doing some resistance, aerobic, and stretching exercises and that would be enough. Someone on a poor diet, even if they seem healthy, has to exercise a lot more to be fit.

It is possible to over exercise. Just because you are healthy and have a lot of stamina doesn't mean you should go out and exercise five times a day. Similarly, people who exercise five times a day to burn off the amount of sugar they have consumed are just as imbalanced. Fruit is an excellent food; I love fruit and think that we could be eating it everyday. However, some people eat too much fruit and have to exercise in order to keep their blood sugar stable. That is almost like being what I call an exercise bulimic.

Do you think that drinking vegetable juice is necessary to succeed on a Raw Diet?
No, I don't think that it is necessary, but I think it is a tremendous adjunct. I think that there is a mistaken notion out there that you are always better off chewing the vegetables and extracting the nutrients and the juices on your own. You can be successful without the vegetable juices; however, in the last 40 years, I have seen many people on raw foods and when they started drinking vegetable juice, it seemed to enhance their state of health.

I don't recommend that you drink excessive amounts of fruit juice. If you are going to drink fruit juice it's better if you dilute them with water. However, if you exercise strenuously, the body is not secreting insulin because your sugar reserves may be a little depleted. In that window after exercising, your body can utilize the fruit sugar without affecting your blood sugar.

The great thing about vegetable juices is that they alkalize your blood. If people eating raw foods seem to have a lot of gas, there is a very good chance their blood pH is not where it should be. Vegetable juices are very alkalizing and can help in this regard.

I have done quite a few long term water fasts. I think in some cases this can be tremendously beneficial, although in many respects, water fasting is misunderstood. When you water fast, symptoms of detox are more severe because you are releasing tremendous amounts of endogenous acid into your blood and it is not exiting the body quickly enough. When you are juice fasting with mostly vegetable juices and some fruit juices, endogenous acid forming material released into your system is being alkalized. It is because of this alkalizing power that vegetable juices can make fasting more comfortable.

A lot of people think water fasting is better because you feel worse. True, it might take a little bit longer, but you can still reap the same results. I've gone as long as five months on juices and felt absolutely wonderful without any problems whatsoever and I got tremendous benefits from it. I don't see anything wrong with juices. When it comes to vegetable juicing, the bottom line indicator to me is that I don't know anybody that lived longer then Norman Walker and he was into juicing.

Just to be clear: I'm not against water fasting. I have personally done eight long term water fasts ranging from 30-50 days each. However, I have heard some unfortunate stories about people being pushed too hard on a water fast when it was unnecessary.

Does the body of a raw food eater handle stress better?
I would say yes, as long as they are doing it correctly. Handling stress also has a lot to do with a person's emotional psychological state of mind, and how much fresh air and exercise they are getting. Don't forget, there must be thousands of different variables in the human body. It's impossible to make a blanket statement. So I would say in most cases of course yes, but it all depends upon the person.

I have had experiences with people that had severe emotional psychological problems. They went on a raw diet and they did 100% better. However, some people still have that tendency, whether it has to do genetics, their way of thinking, or even the thoughts they entertain. If we continue entertaining negative, unhappy, vicious, or violent thoughts, they all become a reality in our life. They become part of what happens to your physiology; physically, emotionally, and psychologically.

Do you believe that Breatharianism is possible?
I have my own opinions about that. It is something that I'd rather not discuss. If I had to discuss it with someone in private I would, but in public I don't want to make any kind of statement.

Do you feel that supplements are necessary for a raw food eater?
Again, I say that there are thousands of variables in the

human body; also, it depends on what you classify as supplements. I just told you about a person with vitamin B-12 deficiency. I definitely didn't think it was necessary for him to go back and eat animal protein. I told him to take a good form of vitamin B-12 and his body responded almost immediately.

I don't believe in high dosage vitamins. At high levels, they act like pharmaceuticals because the human body cannot accept a nutrient at high dosage and thinks it is a chemical. I don't classify enzymes, probiotics, and super green foods as supplements. Supplements heated at low temperatures and taken from whole foods are still, in my mind, food.

In many cases supplementation could be very beneficial. They can help people through transition, long term problems, certain illnesses, and chemical malfunctions. I particularly favor supergreen foods, enzymes and probiotics. I have seen unbelievable results from people using enzymes and probiotics. In cases of tooth abscesses and swollen gums, enzymes and probiotics can heal them within four days.

Enzymes and probiotics can mimic the results of fasting. If you know how to use them, you can clean your system without abstaining from food. As I touched upon before, I had an incident in my own life years ago where I firmly believe that the enzymes and probiotics saved my life. In serious cases, people should have guidance. I never go by anecdotal information alone. What was good for me might not be good for the next person. I look at each person as an individual and try to do a good profile and a personal history so I can best help them; I think that is what everybody should do for themselves.

I have heard you say that many spiritual things happen to the person that becomes a 100% raw food eater. Can you talk about any of those spiritual experiences?

The spiritual life we experience has a lot to do with our internal chemistry. When you eat a raw food diet, you are leaving out just about everything that is not conducive to a healthy physiology. When your body starts cleaning its internal environment and purifying your blood, the way our bodies were designed to do, you are going to become a more spiritually evolved person. You will be developing a super consciousness and opening pathways to be connected spiritually. Your eyes are going to open and you will start seeing the spiritual profoundness we were always meant to see.

Most people eating a bad diet are so polluted. That is one of the reasons why so many fall into all different types of perversions and develop a criminal mentality. I have seen criminal mentalities change when they adopted a better diet. Without even going through counseling they softened and became less aggressive. They start to let go of all the antisocial criminal type of thoughts they were having. By cleaning your blood stream and getting rid of endogenous poisons, your body works better on a cellular level and your brain functions more efficiently. You automatically become a more gentle, unconditionally loving type of person.

One thing I noticed many years ago with myself is that I started to develop a reverence for animals. They felt almost like people to me. When I was a young kid I had a dog. I liked my dog, but not like I *love* my dogs today. I have two dogs and to me they are just as important as a person because they are full of life. Your whole concept, your appraisal of life, your vision of what's taking place on this planet, and your relationship to other people – changes. Everybody is important to you, whether you know them or not and you are more forgiving, even if someone does something nasty. Although you might get upset or angry for a moment or two, the next day the animosity is gone.

So yes, I believe that eating a good diet has a lot to do with your spiritual development. I watch people searching for answers from organized religion or searching spiritually while still eating a bad diet, and I see what a tremendous struggle it is for them. I see how much easier it is for a person that incorporates the type of lifestyle that God meant for us. With this lifestyle, it is much easier to be spiritually connected and to follow the path that we are supposed to walk.

What has a Raw Diet done to your brain (memory)?
There is absolutely no connection, no relationship, to the person I am today and the person I was 45 or 50 years ago. I look back on my young adult life and childhood and see that I am a completely different person. Not that I was a bad person at all, I just can't believe that is who I was.

Even though I'm in the 8th decade of my life, the raw diet continuously allows me to see things clearer and clearer. The more I do this, the more I see how little we know about life. As my eyes open up a little bit more each day, I realize that I don't really know very much at all. There is so much more to learn, especially spiritually of course. If you look around in the world you can see all the chaos. In the Middle East, everybody is killing everybody in the name of God. We each have our own idea about who has the best "religion"; yet I feel there is a natural way to be, beyond all the controversies. I don't want to make any statements that are going to alienate or offend anyone. I believe that God meant for us to evolve and to be much more then we are today.

Do you feel that men should conserve their sperm?
I believe that is another misconception. I think a lot of this

stuff is mystical and esoteric and I don't agree with most of it. Once you get to a level of purity and you evolve spiritually, you don't even have to think along those lines because a person's sexual relationship is going to be based on pure love rather then any kind of lust.

This concept of conserving sperm is something out of eastern philosophy and I think it is misguided. Once you have a true spiritual relationship, you will know what I mean.

People in imbalanced sexual relationships based on lust don't realize they're bankrupting the very essence of their being and they eventually lose their abilities. That is a terrible mistake. If you understand how it was really meant to be, impotency never happens. You can live to be 1000 years old and you will probably still be able to do what you have to do, if you know what I am getting at.

Can someone eliminate all of his or her Sexual Transmitted Diseasess (STD's) on a raw food diet?

Again, I don't make absolute statements, but I would say that if done correctly, it is absolutely possible. It all depends on what a person is doing and what they continue to do. Some people fail because they do not go far enough into cleansing the body. They refuse to do any kind of internal cleansing because they think it is unnatural. Having said that however, a raw diet done correctly is your best chance for getting rid of them.

I don't make any absolute statements because I have seen people fail in all areas of everything. If that wasn't the case, everyone on a raw food diet would live to be 120 or 130.

Is a raw food diet the best way to deal with degenerative diseases?

Done correctly, and including internal cleansing, ABSOLUTE-

LY YES! Everyone should be under the care of a physician; I am not diagnosing or prescribing anything. A raw food diet complementary with medical supervision, is the best way to go.

What is your diet like? How many times a day do you normally eat?

Normally I eat one to two times a day. Some days I just do liquids. So far today, I drank only liquids and will probably continue that the rest of the day. I never really plan my meals; I'm not obsessed with eating and not bondaged in any single way to my food. Some days I might take probiotics and enzymes. I make sure to get all the fatty acids and eat a variety of different produce throughout the week.

All you have to do is think about it. In the natural realm, nobody ate the same day in and day out. They were always able to eat a variety of different foods offering a variety of nutrients. My diet is simple and I rarely deviate. On occasion I might go up to the new raw food restaurant here in New York City and have something. I don't feel as great, but the meals don't make me sick. I like being around people and go there for social reasons.

There is a lot more to being healthy then just what you eat. You have to become a well-rounded person. There many things in my world besides food. I love good music, spending time with my dogs, being with my friends, I enjoy a good movie every once in awhile and going down to the ocean where I run and stretch. My diet is 100% Raw and includes fruits, vegetables, nuts, and seeds. I try not to overeat anything. However, I am not perfect.

I lead a very active life. Many days I put in long hours and follow a very arduous work schedule. I am a married man with a younger family, which comes with a lot of responsibilities. Also, I live in a house on a large piece of property where I try to do all the work myself. There are some days I get so busy that I don't eat. It might be nighttime before I find the time to eat, which is not ideal.

Basically, I stick to my diet, don't eat a lot of food, make sure that I am connecting all the dots by eating a variety of different foods, and I juice. I juice just about every day of the week; it is very important to me. I try not to eat a lot at one sitting. In fact, people that see me eat probably think that I don't eating enough. Every once in awhile I will have a large salad which many might think is small. This is what works best for me. I try to keep myself as stress free as possible. Unfortunately, what I do is very stressful. Daily, I receive an incredible amount of phone calls from really sick people. I know that it is probably taking its toll.

I don't sleep much. I can go without sleep without feeling tired in the morning. I want to emphasize, though, that rest is extremely important and my lack of sleep is possibly one of the worst failures in my life. I'm faring a bit better that the average person would because of my many years on a raw food diet. Sometimes while sleeping, I stay aware of everything going on around me. I am even able to think while sleeping, although I'm not sure if I ever reach a deep REM sleep. As crazy as it might sound, I get a lot of insights during "sleep".

I want to impress upon the reader that a Raw Food Lifestyle is by far the best way to go. There is nothing that can compare. To all the people that have never tried it, did not do well, or did not give it enough time, there is no amount of money on this earth that could equal the value of all the benefits a person could experiences if they take it all the way.

The Raw Foods Lifestyle is the most thrilling, beneficial

path in life, both physically and spiritually, that a person can pursue. It may or may not be easy depending on the individual person. Eating Raw is so dramatic and profound that words can't emphasize enough the good things that can happen. I encourage people who want to try this to understand all the positives and the ramifications, the ups and the downs. Take everything into consideration, but know that being Raw is by far the most rewarding thing a person can do as far as dietary lifestyle is concerned. ✘

It is what you leave out of your diet completely without cheating that heals you. May your journey to reclaiming health be swift and gentle.

INDEX

ABOUT THE AUTHOR

Matt Monarch is a 100% Raw; his diet consists of only raw vegetables, fruits, nuts, and seeds. He is currently the owner of three different health promoting websites.

www.TheRawWorld.com: In partnership with Raw Food Pioneer Dr. Fred Bisci, PhD and 50 year Nutritionist, and Paul Nison, internationally recognized author, speaker and Raw Food Gourmet Health Chef. Matt has co-created this website which sells support tools to help people live free of degenerative disease.

Matt's two other websites are: **www.RawVeganBooks.com** and **www.LivingNutritionals.com**.

After five years of eating a 100% raw food diet, Matt was inspired to write a book called Raw Spirit. He wanted to share information that he thought needed to be out there. Currently, Matt lives in Ojai, California.

NOTES

NOTES

NOTES

NOTES